1998

CHANGING THE PRACTICE OF TEACHER EDUCATION

STANDARDS AND ASSESSMENT AS A LEVER FOR CHANGE

Mary E. Diez, Editor

AACTE
AMERICAN
ASSOCIATION
OF COLLEGES
FOR TEACHER
EDUCATION

Published in cooperation with the *Teaching for Tomorrow* Project at Alverno College

Published in cooperation with the
Teaching for Tomorrow Project at Alverno College

The development of this document
and the *Teaching for Tomorrow* Project at Alverno College
were supported by grants from the Philip Morris Companies Inc.

The American Association of Colleges for Teacher Education is a national,
voluntary association of colleges and universities with undergraduate or
graduate programs to prepare professional educators. The Association supports
programs in data gathering, equity, leadership development, networking,
policy analysis, professional issues, and scholarship.

Copies of
Changing the Practice of Teacher Education:
Standards and Assessment as a Lever for Change
may be ordered from:

AACTE Publications
One Dupont Circle, Suite 610
Washington, DC 20036-1186
http://www.aacte.org

CONTENTS

Part III.
The Change Process: Lessons Learned

PREFACE

■

S even years ago, AACTE published a volume under the title "Changing the Practice of Teacher Education." That monograph addressed issues associated with the professional knowledge base and its role in changing teacher preparation in a variety of institutions. We make use of the same rubric now to present a volume addressing the role of standards and assessment in transforming the way teacher educators think about developing the next generations of teachers. Intervening years have seen an evolution in the thinking of educators and policymakers, moving from concern with the foundational knowledge underlying teacher education toward a focus on the effective use of that knowledge in the current context of standards and assessment.

Today's education reform agendas are especially dependent on the concept of assessment, intended not only to gauge student learning and teacher development, but more importantly, to help deepen understandings of educational standards and to transform support for the learner. How will these expectations for assessment be realized in teacher education programs? What is involved in the process of helping teacher educators take on the challenges of this expanded focus on assessment? And what are the contextual issues that surround efforts by individual campuses in the midst of a national dialogue about assessment—from national test proposals to local mandates?

This volume takes a significant step toward helping educators and policymakers understand and respond to this challenge. It presents a complex tapestry that interweaves experiences of individual teacher education programs with relevant issues probed by a panel of national leaders in teacher assessment. This volume also provides clear observation and guidance in decisions about assessment to be made at state and institutional levels.

With much admiration for the significant work undertaken by the institutions whose efforts around standards and assessment are profiled here, we offer this monograph. We invite readers to join us in addressing this challenge.

David G. Imig
Chief Executive Officer, AACTE

ACKNOWLEDGMENTS

A central message of this volume—that change requires the collaborative efforts of many persons who share a common vision—also reflects the experience of working with the *Teaching for Tomorrow* Project and the production of this volume. Diane Eidman, of Philip Morris Companies Inc., supported both the original project that allowed Alverno to work with other teacher education programs interested in using standards and assessment as a lever for reform and the development of this volume as a resource for policymakers and teacher educators. Along the way, her colleagues at Philip Morris, including Karen Brosius, Kitty Breen, and Henry Fernandez, also provided encouragement and advice.

Adding to the richness of this volume as a resource are the many persons in the teacher education community who contributed their time and effort. Those who participated in the dialogue brought important insights from their work with NCATE, INTASC, the National Board for Professional Teaching Standards, and the measurement community. Those who described their experiences with local efforts toward reform provided a concrete picture of the many ways in which change unfolds. Alverno faculty involved over time with the *Teaching for Tomorrow* Project worked with their colleagues across the other institutions to capture patterns that emerge in the change process. These colleagues and friends contributed to the design of the volume in thoughtful and interactive ways.

Carol Smith, Senior Director for Professional Issues at AACTE, guided the development of this volume in her quiet, effective way, providing encouragement, organizational support, and editorial assistance. Kristin McCabe coordinated all technical aspects of production, with assistance from Beth Foxwell in the editing process. These AACTE staff members continue the association's tradition of solid, professional service.

■

Mary E. Diez

INTRODUCTION

Mary E. Diez

This volume brings together resources for the reform of teacher education not often found in one place. It begins with a discussion of conceptual issues related to the impact of standards and assessment on teacher education, laying the foundation for the description of seven teacher education institutions that have engaged in using standards and assessment to guide their approaches to reform. These descriptions illustrate the necessarily local nature of implementation of reform efforts, even with a common set of principles. The volume concludes with a set of reflections on the change process—what it takes to initiate change, support it, and sustain it—drawn from the experience of the seven teacher education programs and their institutions. Because of its combination of theoretical perspectives and concrete experience, this volume can serve as a useful guide to policymakers, researchers, and teacher educators.

The success of teacher education reform depends upon each of the aspects described above—conceptual principles and frameworks to guide the reform, attention to local conditions and cultures, and ongoing reflection to learn from the process even as it is taking place. In recent years, some of those concerned with the need to reform teacher education have begun with thoughtful conceptualizations of what ought to be, responding to problems as they perceived them. These researchers and teacher educators have created whole visions of teacher education reform in theory and offered them to others as blueprints for action. The proposal to move teacher education to a "professional development school" (PDS) model is a case in point. To the degree that local implementation of a PDS approach has been thoughtfully undertaken, guided by the principles rather than structural detail, and adapted through experience and reflection on that experience, the PDS vision has had a positive impact on teacher education reform. But when some institutions merely adopt the label, rather than changing their practice, and other institutions focus more on the details of a structure for the PDS than on goals it is intended to achieve, the impact of the vision can be compromised.

This volume describes a contrasting approach to teacher education reform. The institutions described herein began not with a complete vision, but with their own institutions and their own experience, looking through the lens of principles about standards and assessment. They drew upon theoretical frameworks related to teaching and learning, informed by specific problems from their own experience, and used the experience of practice to build a conceptualization to guide that practice. Their processes for engaging in change were designed with local situations and constraints in mind, and their designs offer contrasting methods of approaching the identification of outcomes (or abilities, or strands, or standards—even the names vary), the design of learning and assessment experiences, and the developing of strong connections with P–12 schools. Critical to each of the programs described in this volume is a commitment to discourse as a means of synthesizing frameworks drawn from both theory and experience. The result is a model of teacher education that is organic and responsive to the unique characteristics of the institution and its community.

The *Teaching for Tomorrow* Project

In 1993, the Philip Morris Companies Inc. awarded a grant to the faculty at Alverno College to support their work with a small network of teacher education programs. Across 14 states with Philip Morris Company sites, 40 programs were invited to submit applications to be part of the program in fall 1993. Eleven applications were received and four sites were chosen in February 1994; among the four institutions selected were three that continued with the process for the full three years of funding: Clayton College and State University (Ga.), the University of Northern Colorado, and Winston-Salem State University (N.C.).

The *Teaching for Tomorrow* Project provided support from both liberal arts and teacher education faculty at Alverno College for teams of educators from the *Teaching for Tomorrow* institutions as they redesigned their programs to prepare teachers. The *Teaching for Tomorrow* institutions agreed to undertake reform by clarifying the outcomes of their programs, developing performance assessment processes to develop and document the development of student learning outcomes, developing strategies to involve faculty across the institution and in P–12 schools in the reform effort, and designing an evaluation plan to guide continuous improvement efforts.

In the first year, the four institutions began their work through participation in a two-week program at Alverno. Teams of six liberal-arts and teacher education faculty from each institution came to Alverno in summer 1994 for the college's Assessment Workshop for college and P–12 educators. This week-long workshop provided a conceptual base for the identification of outcomes, learning experiences to develop those outcomes, and assessment strategies to both foster and document student development. The teams remained on campus for an additional week, working on the conceptualization or refinement of teacher education outcomes for their individual institutions. They used a variety of resources to guide their work, including the propositions of the National Board for Professional Teaching Standards, the model standards developed by the Interstate New Teacher Assessment and Support Consortium, and the Alverno teacher education model.

During the 1994–95 school year, Alverno teams (one liberal arts faculty member and one teacher education faculty member) worked with the four institutions in a variety of ways: facilitating small group sessions, providing workshops, critiquing materials and plans, and the like. The Alverno team also maintained close communication with the institutional teams between visits, responding to their needs and questions as they moved through the process of reform.

The visits from the Alverno facilitators supported the work of the *Teaching for Tomorrow* team on each campus. In three out of the four sites, the local teams met on a regular basis and engaged the support of the institution's administration; they involved other faculty in the development of a common vision and common language, leading to readiness for engagement in the tasks of creating coherence across courses and developing an assessment plan. At Winston-Salem State University, for example, faculty across the institution began to meet on a monthly basis in interdisciplinary "satellite groups" to explore the meaning of the abilities that they had determined as graduation expectations. The entire faculty agreed to begin to develop three abilities—communication, problem solving, and critical thinking—across the curriculum. At Clayton College & State University, the weekly meeting of the interdisciplinary team responsible for the development of the middle school teacher education program guided the clarification of the outcomes for the program and the development of an assessment plan. At the University of Northern Colorado, a much larger institution than the other two, faculty from liberal arts and from the Professional Teacher Education Programs (PTEPs) in elementary, middle, secondary and P–12 areas met on a regular basis to clarify their outcomes in relationship to the Colorado standards and to develop performance assessments to guide and document student growth.

The fourth institution was unable to overcome what its members perceived as insurmountable difficulties on its campus—namely, seeing the economic climate of the state as a barrier to faculty investing energy in the review of their programs through the design of clear outcomes and assessment measures. There had been little progress in preparation for the first visit of the Alverno team in December, so when the local team chose not to schedule any visits for spring, the director and the team made a mutual decision to end their involvement in the project.

During the 1995–96 and 1996–97 school years, the Alverno faculty continued the visits, tailoring the workshops/consultations to the needs of the institutions. A formal plan for evaluation of the program's impact on students and graduates was developed as well. In addition, the Alverno team supported each institution's work with P–12 schools, again providing assistance as appropriate.

In addition to the site visits, the group as a whole convened four more times—brief meetings at AACTE Annual Meetings, and extended retreats in summer 1995 and spring 1996. Presentations about the project were made at AACTE Annual Meetings and AAHE Assessment Conferences as well, with considerable audience interest in the work of the project. Each presentation consisted of a panel about the project and the work on the campuses and break-out sessions where audience members could interact with one of the *Teaching for Tomorrow* teams and their Alverno colleagues.

A climate of trust among the group led to constructive criticism and the sharing of common problems or questions, e.g., how to create experiences and assessments that develop the abilities sought in the program; how to create rubrics that support development rather than simply "sort" students into achievement levels; and how to use feedback and self-assessment to promote growth. New issues emerged during this work. For example, in the summer retreat, the group recognized the need to examine and probe diversity issues both for themselves and for their students, and focused on an examination of their teacher education outcomes in relationship to the development of candidates' ability to integrate many cultures into their curricula and to work effectively with diverse learners.

At the end of the three-year process, each of the institutions had developed clear outcomes to guide its programs, reviewed and revised curriculum, developed assessment plans, and published handbooks for faculty and students. Some of their experiences are captured in Part II of this volume.

To expand the experience base for this monograph, the *Teaching for Tomorrow* team at Alverno identified several additional teacher education programs with similar experiences to the *Teaching for Tomorrow* Project institutions. Some of these institutions had worked with Alverno faculty in other settings, or their work was known to Alverno faculty. In some cases, they had undertaken their reform effort as an institutional focus; in others, they were part of state efforts to use standards and assessments in reforming teacher education.

The Outline of This Book

This volume has three major sections. In Part I, *The Role of Standards and Assessment: A Dialogue,* seven individuals representing various viewpoints and experience bases contribute to a rich discussion of the standards and assessment movement in relationship to teacher education reform. Themes from this section not only highlight the philosophical positions behind the standards and assessment movement but address equity concerns, legal issues, and psychometric concerns as well as policy applications.

Part II, *Using Standards and Assessment to Reform Teacher Education: Seven Examples,* provides examples of practice that attempt to put flesh on the conceptual bones. Included are descriptions of the work of faculty at the *Teaching for Tomorrow* institutions and Alverno College, along with contributions from Ashland University (Ohio), Asbury College (Ky.), and Central Missouri State University. The institutions range from small liberal arts colleges to medium- and large-sized public and private institutions. Although there are seven institutions represented in this section, nine articles are included to capture the experiences of varied teacher educators in the process of reform.

To develop the final section, *The Change Process: Lessons Learned,* members of the *Teaching for Tomorrow* faculty team from Alverno College reflected on their experience with working in the project and drew upon the experiences of the seven institutions described in Part II. They organized these reflections to assist readers to examine what is necessary to begin a change process, the supports needed to continue it, and the institutionalization required to sustain it over time.

Who Can Use This Book?

This volume can be useful to three audiences: policymakers, researchers, and teacher educators. To those responsible for education policy and those whose funding decisions influence policy, it can be of particular value. As Vickers notes in the dialogue on standards and assessment, policymakers rarely have the luxury of seeing in advance the results of their decisions. With the insights presented in this volume, policymakers may avoid the traps of mandating change without necessary supports and of focusing on structures before determining the purposes the structures are meant to achieve.

The rich experience of the seven institutions in this volume can suggest areas for future research. In the experiences of these groups, researchers might find initial answers to the questions asked by many states: What will be the impact of standards and assessment on teacher preparation? Why are some institutions successful in implementing performance-based programs while others are not? How will students who complete performance-based programs use their experience in their own teaching and assessing of their students?

Finally, this volume may be useful to teacher educators seeking support for change. With many states moving toward performance-based licensure, the various types of institutions represented in this volume reinforce the point that there is no one structure that all teacher education programs should implement, nor is there a single kind of institution in which change can occur. The local development of high-quality teacher education programs remains the responsibility of each teacher education faculty. The experience of these seven institutions suggests some common lessons that can guide faculty in other institutions in their reflection on their own change process.

PART I

The Role of Standards and Assessment: A Dialogue

Introduction

■

Mary E. Diez

Teacher quality is at the heart of education reform. From the 1980s reports *A Nation at Risk* and *A Nation Prepared* to the 1996 report *What Matters Most: Teaching for America's Future* by the National Commission on Teaching & America's Future, teaching emerges as central to improving America's schools.

In a metaphor that only partly conveys the importance of standards and assessment to teacher quality, *What Matters Most* describes accreditation, licensing, and certification as a "three-legged stool of teacher quality." Clearly, in the past 15 years, the National Council for the Accreditation of Teacher Education (NCATE), the Interstate New Teacher Assessment and Support Consortium (INTASC), and the National Board for Professional Teaching Standards have helped to focus the agenda of teacher education and teaching practice on what teachers need to know and be able to do. In addition, all three have engaged in the development of new ways to assess teacher knowledge and practice, specifically through performance assessment.

NCATE's redesign in the mid-1980s focused first on what was called the "knowledge base" of teaching, seeking to support the recognition of teaching as a profession. The more recent term, "conceptual framework," recognizes the integration of knowledge and practice in the design of coherent programs to develop and assess individual teacher education candidates. NCATE itself focuses on assuring that teacher preparation institutions have the structure and processes in place to promote and ensure the development of individual candidates. With the identification of state interest in performance-based licensure, NCATE has become increasingly clear in its expectation that teacher preparation programs assess candidates using multiple modes and methods across the program.

INTASC, initially formed in the mid-1980s by California and Connecticut to share their developing work in assessment and to follow Lee Shulman's work for the National Board, has grown to a consortium of more than 30 states, under the Council of Chief State School Officers. In 1990, INTASC took on the task of developing Board-compatible standards for initial licensure, publishing the draft of the model standards in 1992 and continuing to move forward with a testing/assessment framework that can be adopted by states for basic skills testing, as well as assessment of content and pedagogical knowledge to determine readiness for teaching and to evaluate teaching practice during an induction or internship year. Pilots of the portfolio assessment in mathematics and language arts are underway.

The National Board grew out of a proposal in *A Nation Prepared* (1986), again as a strategy to support the professionalization of teaching. Built upon a vision of teaching outlined in five propositions, the board has developed standards—for subject areas and the developmental level of the learner—in relationship to 36 certificate areas. Six certificates are currently being offered, through an assessment process in which teachers create portfolios of their work with learners and respond to Assessment Center Exercises that tap into teacher thinking.

Across these three "legs" of the stool, as well as in the development of teacher education policy in states and in the expectations for teachers outlined by subject area associations, standards and assessment have emerged as a powerful lever for change. How positive is the focus on standards and assessment? What problems or issues need to be examined in relationship to each? What response should a responsible teacher educator make to these efforts?

Working with the American Association of Colleges for Teacher Education, the *Teaching for Tomorrow* Project team from Alverno College brought together a group of individuals with perspectives on standards and assessment issues (see *About the Contributors* at the end of this volume). Through a series of interviews conducted in 1996-97, the team created a virtual dialogue among these seven leaders.

■

References

Carnegie Forum on Education and the Economy: Task Force on Teaching as a Profession. (1986). *A nation prepared: Teachers for the 21ˢᵗ century.* New York: Author.

National Commission on Excellence in Education. (1983). *A nation at risk.* Washington, DC: U.S. Department of Education.

National Commission on Teaching & America's Future. (1996). *What matters most: Teaching for America's future.* New York: Author.

The Role of Standards and Assessment: A Dialogue

Linda Darling-Hammond, Mary E. Diez, Pamela Moss,
Raymond Pecheone, Diana Pullin, William D. Schafer,
and Lelia Vickers

Editor's Note: In the following dialogue, several organizations are referenced by abbreviated names. A brief key may be useful:
- *INTASC* – Interstate New Teacher Assessment and Support Consortium
- *National Board*, or *NBPTS* – National Board for Professional Teaching Standards
- *National Commission*, or *NCTAF* – National Commission on Teaching & America's Future
- *NCATE* – National Council for Accreditation of Teacher Education

1.   Let's begin with an overall question: Is the development of standards and performance assessment across the continuum of teacher preparation a good thing?

William Schafer: It seems to me that not just in teacher preparation but in all areas of education, there is a real lack of defined standards. We lack very specific standards about what the outcomes of education should be. In all areas, we should be working to define standards, then evaluating them somehow to sanction them—and the sanctioning process should include the opportunity to continually revise them. I think this should be done in a public and open way so that all stakeholders have an opportunity to participate.

If we become serious about standards and assessment, then we will find them debated, expanded, paraphrased, and used. The current lack of both public and professional impact of standards and assessment is the result of our not having very many meaningful decisions made using them.

Diana Pullin: I think unless the standards discussion involves a broad range of policymakers, educators, and consumers, it won't be a particularly meaningful discussion. Certainly members of the teaching profession have to play the most significant role in those discussions. But, unless public policymakers are involved and a diverse group of consumers of educational services are involved, I think the standards and the assessments are going to be open to considerable criticism.

Mary Diez: One of the major impacts of the work of NCATE, INTASC, and the National Board, as well as the work in states and learned societies, has been the sparking of a serious dialogue about what constitutes good teaching. In fact, that may be the most important role of standards—to lay out a vision of teaching in a public way so that all in the profession can contribute to its critique and refinement. In that sense, the development of standards is directly related to the development of teaching as a profession.

Raymond Pecheone: The commitment to standards-based reform is very strong in the majority of states, now working on setting common standards for both teachers and students. Overall, this movement has the potential to pay big dividends but I would like to register a few caveats. The appeal of standards is that they are derived by establishing a consensus about teaching and they serve to focus the profession on those skills and abilities that are most related to learning. However, states have engaged in a variety of codification systems that had little effect on student learning (e.g., the competency-based movement and objectives-based curriculum reform). The potential of a standards-based system is that it pays attention to both the knowledge and the skills a teacher needs to impact learning. We haven't seen this potential developed before.

For teachers to make the link between learning and practice, they need to have the opportunity to systematically examine and evaluate student work in relation to their teaching throughout their careers. Conventional systems of course-counting in higher education and state licensure, and one-shot professional development offerings for teachers, do not work and must be changed if we are going to provide meaningful support to teachers who believe in the standards but need help putting them into practice.

Another concern is that standards may serve to limit our understanding of the field and serve as barriers to new knowledge in the profession. This can easily happen when states tie high-stakes assessments to standards. Often a single instrument—a paper-and-pencil test, for example—serves as the sole measure of the standards. Given the limitations of a single assessment methodology, standards can become trivialized and static. What is needed is a process whereby standards are continually rethought and revised. Additionally, assessment systems must be broad-based and incorporate multiple assessment strategies more accurately to measure the intent of the standards.

Pamela Moss: The development of standards and performance assessments can be a means for widespread dialogue, across contexts and levels of the educational system, about what constitutes good teaching. Moreover, the dialogue can be based in concrete examples of teaching practice that the performance assessments provide. While it may be (relatively) easy to reach consensus at the level of generality of most standards documents, that consensus may hide significant differences at the level of actual practice. Performance assessments and other cases of teaching practice force us to consider the meaning of the standards in light of the contingencies of a particular teaching/learning circumstance. Such concrete examples both illustrate and challenge the standards in productive ways. Ideally, consideration of general standards and concrete examples is an ongoing dialectical process.

There are dangers inherent in standards and assessment, however, one of which is to confuse standards with standardization. In the extreme, this risks promoting a narrow view of teaching and learning that excludes other thoughtful perspectives and that undermines the ability of a field to evolve in light of new experience and understanding. If the standards- and assessment-based reform movement is to remain a positive force, it will have to promote an ongoing, open dialogue that continually challenges current perspectives in light of new experience, and that enables both the assessment and the standards to evolve.

Linda Darling-Hammond: What could be a very good thing is creating a real coherence in the learning opportunities that teachers have available to them beginning with preservice teacher education and continuing throughout the career. In the past, most of the tacit standards that have existed for teaching have not viewed teaching as interactive with learning. Teaching is not just the formulaic demonstration of a set of "canned" teaching behaviors, which are performed without attention to whether children are learning or not. New standards and assessments are beginning to make clear the connections between teaching as decision-making and learning.

But there are also aspects of standard-setting that one needs to be careful about. For example, standards and assessments need to be used to develop individual teachers and to move the field ahead but not to become gatekeepers that reduce the diversity in the teaching force, that reduce access to teaching for committed people who want to learn to teach. We also have to be extremely careful that we don't create assessments that favor a dominant culture in ways that are not really related to high-quality teaching but to ideologies or viewpoints about teaching that fail to acknowledge valid forms of teaching which are more prevalent in some communities than others.

Lelia Vickers: When you begin to look at the three sets of standards that we're all trying to work with now (INTASC, National Board, NCATE), I don't know that there is enough diversity represented in any of them. It appears that most standards represent "a Eurocentric model" that can be described as linear rather than holistic. Certain patterns of learning are reflected in such a model that are not inherent in all learners. If the Eurocentric model is used for all standards, some students will continue to be disadvantaged in the assessment process. As demographics change and more students of color are in the classroom, not only must the standards respond to diverse learning needs, but the teaching and assessment methods must also reflect that diversity. There must be more than one way to demonstrate competence and mastery. The cultural context must be considered.

2. *At the heart of standards for teaching must be a conceptualization of teaching itself. What is good teaching?*

Raymond Pecheone: I believe that the framework for good teaching is captured in the work of NCATE, INTASC, the National Board, and individual states' standards-based reforms. Essentially these standards taken together delineate the key aspects of professional practice: planning and preparation, creating a learning environment, effective instruction and professional responsibilities. Moreover, those organizations are attempting to use these frameworks to establish levels of professional practice within each stage of a teacher's career: preparation (NCATE), induction (INTASC), and advanced certification (National Board).

One danger of adopting the standards framework as our definition of "good teaching" is that standards represent the current consensus about good teaching and have the potential to stifle other views of effective teaching. This phenomenon will be further exacerbated if high-stakes assessments are linked to standards. For example, new assessments (e.g., the

National Board portfolios) may be tilted to privilege constructivist forms of teaching to the exclusion of other strategies that might be more or equally appropriate given a certain context.

William Schafer: We would like good teaching to produce learning and that, it seems to me, is our criterion. It focuses on product instead of process. What we have is a fundamental, basic criterion of student learning and the processes that enhance learning. I don't think we know as much about that as we would like to. We don't know very much about the variation of effectiveness, or successful educational processes across different contexts, given different students and different teachers.

Lelia Vickers: I don't think it's possible to answer "what is good teaching" with one answer. I think there are standards, and parameters, and some information that is probably very objective. But then there are other areas that are going to be related to a specific population, or a specific individual, and the *results* that come from actual teaching. These determine whether or not it is really good teaching. In other words, did learning occur? We must have individuals who understand the experience and challenges and are willing to sit in various settings and work collaboratively to develop assessments and not depend totally on the "experts."

Linda Darling-Hammond: I think we know good teaching in part by its results—that is, students do learn and grow. But we also know it by its processes. I think both are important. The process has to be defensible, it has to be thoughtful, it has to be humane, it has to be attentive to student ideas and concerns as well as to curriculum goals that the teacher and school want students to learn. As teachers, we want students to make academic gains but we must also help them deal with the lessons that life is putting in front of them at the same time.

Mary Diez: Many states are suggesting that teachers should be judged not against a set of standards for effective teaching, but against the effectiveness of their teaching on students. While I think we have a long way to go to be able to assess the results of teaching practice, we need to be working on that. Too often teachers and others in school settings accept as unchangeable factors that reduce the impact of their teaching. Shouldn't working for optimal conditions for learning be considered part of teaching, as much as lessons planned and delivered?

3.   *How does student learning get considered fairly?*

Pamela Moss: Student learning is one important indicator of good teaching, but clearly not the only important indicator. Problems arise with any assessment system when we look for simplistic answers that focus on one indicator at a time. Whether the news is good or bad, we have no understanding of how or why the results occurred. Information about student learning should be located within a rich understanding of teaching practices, available resources, students' background, school and district culture, community support, and so on. I don't think it is productive to separate questions about teaching practice from student learning or from an understanding of the context in which it occurs.

Raymond Pecheone: There will always be methods and objectives that work for certain children and not other children. It takes multiple data sources over time.

There needs to be a connection between the standards that we use for teacher preparation and the standards we use for licensure and certification of teachers. Performance-based data is evidence of whether we are effectively preparing new teachers for the challenges of the next century. We need to move away from course-counting and toward ensuring that students have met standards through the collection of systematic evidence.

4.   *How do we use standards coupled with professional judgment in the identification of good teaching?*

Diana Pullin: I think it's absolutely essential that there be a coherent and coordinated approach taken to defining good teaching and defining how to set standards, what those standards ought to be and how to assess performance. I think one of the reasons that the educational profession is most subject to criticism by members of the public at-large has been the inability to articulate a common shared set of expectations about good teaching and how to assess good teaching. If we cannot present the public a clear and coherent articulation of good teaching and how to assess good teaching, we will play right into the hands of those who argue that education is not a true profession.

Pamela Moss: Standards, thoughtfully applied, provide us with a conceptual framework—a way of looking at teaching practice—to illuminate and value significant features. Thus, they play an important role in the evaluation of teaching. Given the complexities of teaching, such thoughtful application of standards requires professional judgment. Moreover, professional judgment plays an additional, crucial role, by attending to those aspects of practice which are not illuminated by the standards, but which may be important to consider because they challenge existing standards and/or suggest other possible standards. Again, a vital standards and assessment system is one based in continual critical reflection so that the standards and assessment system can evolve in light of new understanding and experience.

Linda Darling-Hammond: I think we do know good teaching by the thoughtful application of professional standards, but those standards are not uniformities. They're really broad principles of practice that can only be seen and interpreted by expert professionals who can look at practices against a knowledge base and make judgments about whether the kinds of decisions being made are appropriate given both the knowledge base and the context.

Mary Diez: Of course, if we find good teaching—in terms of results with students—that seems not to fit with the standards, that's a signal that the standards need review.

5. *What is the vision of teaching embedded in the standards of NCATE, INTASC, and the National Board?*

Mary Diez: It's a vision that holds that all children are capable of much more development than we have sometimes given them credit for. Teaching ought to unlock the potential in those children; provide opportunities for growth that recognize individual backgrounds and histories and differences and talents. It's a vision that basically says the role of the teacher is very important for creating a classroom climate and environment where learning can happen even if the other environments in that child's life militate against learning.

Lelia Vickers: One of the really important factors in this vision is the attention to cultural diversity. We must look at how differences and sensitivity to differences permeates the curriculum. As teachers prepare for the National Board, a cultural component must be provided to ensure that diverse cultural experiences are integrated into portfolios.

6. *What is good assessment?*

William Schafer: One aspect of good assessment is that it not be a surprise. By explaining to students what the assessment is going to consist of, we really direct their study. If their preparation is efficient and it's focused on what we want to achieve, they're not guessing about what we've told them.

It seems to me that any assessment program should be judged just like an educational program, according to explicit, public criteria. I could suggest a beginning set of four criteria that might be developed further as a result of an open and consensus-building process that involves appropriate stakeholders. Those possible standards for an assessment program are: first, explicit and comprehensive standards that describe the curriculum have been developed and disseminated; second, procedures exist that are valid and reliable and can be used to assess the degree to which each student's learning has met the standards; third, the procedures are used systematically to evaluate how well student performance matches the program's expectations; and fourth, the information is analyzed and interpreted to document both student and program success and to improve the quality of the program.

Good assessment in the '90s is assessment that provides policymakers with a valid measure of performance and at the same time provides valuable information to educators that informs us about the learning process. Often the hallmark of a good assessment system is its use of a variety of assessment strategies to evaluate teaching, which may include paper-and-pencil tests, performance assessments, observations, interviews, and so on.

Pamela Moss: Good assessment cannot be usefully described in the abstract. One has to begin by asking the purpose of an assessment and whether that purpose should be served. In the context of teaching, assessments serve a variety of purposes, from high-stakes assessments that enable a licensure or certification decision to lower-stakes assessments intended to assess learning in a particular course, enable ongoing mentoring, or otherwise support professional development through personal reflection and collegial interaction. Each purpose brings a different set of contingencies to assessment development and evaluation—no one system will serve all purposes equally well. A good assessment is one that enables sound decisions or interpretations in light of its purposes, one where the effects or consequences of using the assessment for all stakeholders have been illuminated and evaluated, and one that evolves in light of ongoing critical reflection about its meaning and its effects.

Within the literature on educational assessment (and educational research more broadly), there exist useful general statements about validity theory and detailed examples of validity practice intended to develop "good assessments." Examples relevant to teaching include research and development agendas undertaken by Alverno College, by Connecticut, by INTASC, and by the National Board. None of these differing programs of validity research represents an "ideal" set of practices, but they illustrate how thoughtful people use empirical evidence to grapple with the complex (epistemological, ethical, political, and practical) issues involved in the assessment of teaching for various purposes.

Linda Darling-Hammond: I think good assessment is an authentic representation of the actual activities or tasks we want to measure or assess competence in. The tasks are chosen in such a way that they also capture several kinds of knowledge and skills that we know people will need to have developed to succeed in the enterprise they are pursuing.

Second, good assessment is structured in such a way that candidates have several points of access to good performance. A task should not be so narrow that there is only one pathway to success. It should be open to a variety of pathways that represent the way people would come at that task in the real world. There will be multiple approaches to problems and there should be multiple solutions to most good performance tasks.

Mary Diez: I think good assessment fulfills multiple purposes for different audiences. It first of all provides information for the learner and in the case of younger children, the learner and the parents of the learner. It provides information about their learning that can help them move to the next step. It gives learners an awareness of what they did well so they can do it again, and of what they didn't do so well so they can put some focus on it and grow.

Then assessment is also very important for teachers so they can improve what they're doing. Ongoing assessment helps the teacher to see what wasn't clear or what didn't work for all learners. Thus it helps the teacher to plan.

A third purpose for assessment is improvement of programs. Assessment results can provide information related to curriculum development at the building, district, or even state level.

Lelia Vickers: Good assessment is a combination of assessments. There will most always be written requirements where students are given the opportunity to express content. Whether multiple-choice or essay, there will be some assessment where the student actually puts in writing what he or she has learned in a particular course.

What I find equally significant in teaching is the opportunity to allow students to demonstrate that they can apply what has been taught. I just don't think there is any way one can teach and not put in those kinds of assessments where students actually demonstrate and integrate what has been learned. There must be a variety of opportunities to demonstrate one's effectiveness as a teacher in the classroom. Teachers must assume responsibility for learning.

Raymond Pecheone: The INTASC effort is an example of a system that is attempting to model a combined approach. It proposes that teacher candidates take a paper-and-pencil performance assessment (not a multiple-choice test) upon graduation. During the first year of employment, beginning teachers would complete a portfolio to evaluate their performance over time.

In structuring the INTASC assessments, three key features are present: 1) all assessment tasks are linked to a set of common standards; 2) the assessment tasks are situated in real-world problems or activities that should be highly relevant to the examinees' experiences; and 3) the scoring criteria or rubrics are understood by both the scorers and the examinees. Moreover, these assessments are designed to be a catalyst for new learning, and participation in the assessment should provide a basis for learning to occur.

The experience of candidates taking the National Board assessments supports continuing learning. Board candidates continue to celebrate the educational benefits of the Board assessments as one of the most meaningful professional development experiences of their lives.

7. *Do standards for performance require new approaches to assessment?*

Pamela Moss: Clearly, the kinds of standards developed by INTASC or the National Board require complex, performance-based evidence about teaching practice, and evaluating this evidence requires similarly complex human judgments. Such assessments, particularly when used in a large-scale, high-stakes context, present knotty technical problems that push the boundaries of conventional practice in educational measurement. While I think it is possible to solve (many of) the technical problems without straying too far from the field of psychometrics—the National Board assessments being an existence proof—I think there are important questions to raise about the kinds of assessment practices promoted by psychometric theory.

One argument that I've made elsewhere goes something like this: In evaluating teaching performance, conventional psychometric practices require readers to work independently, evaluating one performance at a time, blind to the teacher's performance on other exercises. However, current calls for reform in the professional development and practice of teachers suggest that successful teachers integrate complex evidence about their students' learning and the context in which they work, that they engage in ongoing critical reflection about their own teaching practices, and that they work as members of active learning communities. And so, there is a disjunction between the practices in which readers engage and what is expected of the teachers whose work they are evaluating.

This disjunction suggests two questions. Would a sound (perhaps sounder) interpretation result if readers were allowed to consider *all* the evidence available about a candidate and engage in dialogue with one another about the performances? What would the impact be on readers' professional development if they were encouraged to engage in a process that more closely reflects the habits of mind and practice that the assessment is intended to evaluate and promote? Validity research programs underway, for instance, at Alverno College and at INTASC are providing evidence that addresses these questions across quite different contexts of assessment.

Raymond Pecheone: The move to include performance assessment as one component of a good assessment system has fostered changes in the way we think about the design of assessments, the scoring of assessments, and the reliability and validity of the assessment process.

In the design phase, tasks are identified that are both representative of the standards and relevant to the job of teaching. Unlike multiple-choice items, tasks are complex and multidimensional and require many more revisions and small pilot tests before they are ready for a large-scale field trial. Task development is labor intensive and requires considerable expertise from practitioners to situate the task in an authentic teaching experience. What's new in the design of performance assessment is the amount of preparation needed on the front end to design a good assessment.

Scoring of performances is also more complex; there are no right and wrong answers, but often a range of more acceptable answers and less acceptable answers. Procedures for scoring are contextualized and created simultaneously with the design of the assessment tasks. Therefore, assessments that look similar may use very different approaches to scoring. For example, the National Board uses a task-based scoring process and INTASC uses a process that integrates performances across tasks, leading to a single portfolio score. In performance assessment, scoring is not uniform and many customized and different approaches are used. Therefore, the validity of the scoring process must be established at the same time as the design of the performance tasks is being formulated.

The psychometric properties of performance tasks still rest on traditional understanding about the reliability and validity of assessments; however, these assessments do pose many interesting dilemmas to psychometricians. Because performance assessments yield candidate responses in varied degrees of appropriateness, achieving consistency in judgments across raters is more difficult. Designers of performance assessment are continually refining the scoring process to improve reliability without sacrificing validity. Validity evidence also is more challenging, since performance assessment has little history behind it. There is not yet a body of research to support the assessment processes; therefore, it is the responsibility of test designers to conduct research that informs the profession about the validity of the interpretation of the assessment results. Recognizing the need for research, INTASC and the National Board have initiated a wide array of studies to examine the reliability and validity of their groundbreaking assessments.

8. *The assumptions we make about assessment can make a difference in how we apply it. Some people talk about old mindsets that get in the way of new approaches. How do you see those mindsets operating?*

Mary Diez: In the Milwaukee mathematics assessment, the school district published the questions in the newspaper so people could see what we're expecting of kids. That action challenged two old mindsets: first, what will be tested needs to be secret; and second, that assessment is separate from teaching and learning.

It makes sense to focus on secrecy when it's the answers to questions rather than the process of thinking you value. But the very best assessments make explicit what students (or teachers) need to do with what they know.

If assessment is totally separate from learning, then it can't really impact or influence learning. Kids who are in plays, musical performances, or football practice what they're going to perform. We need to think about teaching, learning, and assessment in that same way. If we have clear standards, then learners can practice towards those standards. Asking students to learn how to do what the standard demands leads to knowing and doing, not just disconnected knowing.

Finally, there's also a testing mindset that assumes that the tester knows all the answers before giving the test and the student's role is to memorize those correct answers. One problem with item analysis in standardized testing is that one has no way of knowing the reasons behind an incorrect answer. The correct process in mathematics with a slight computation error, for example, may lead to a wrong answer.

Performance assessment is built on a different assumption—namely, that we don't know exactly what the possibilities are even if we have a sense of some of the criteria that should be used.

Raymond Pecheone: As a state test director, I admit that we certainly have helped set testing apart from instruction. If good assessment is connected to learning and the purpose of assessment is not simply to label students but to help everyone learn, then many of these old mindsets must be changed. In the context of new assessments, change means that we do a much better job in designing tests that inform teachers and parents about what a student knows and doesn't know. State reporting of scores should be more than a horse race indicating who scored highest and lowest; instead, scores should inform educators and the public about what students know and are able to do.

Therefore, scoring must not be secretive but be deliberately designed to be more transparent. A transparent scoring system enables students, teachers, and parents to understand student performance in light of exemplars that are developed to define each score point. If we begin to demystify testing, then many of these old mindsets can be changed and testing may be viewed in a more positive light as an integral part of learning.

Linda Darling-Hammond: Policymakers, practitioners, parents, and members of the public have been socialized in particular ways based on their own experiences as students. I think one of the ways we help people understand how valuable open and authentic assessment can be is by giving them an experience of it. We've got to figure out ways to give policymakers and other adults experiences of good assessment so that they can then understand how it can support others.

Another thing we've got to grapple with are the uses of assessment. The reason we have a lot of emphasis on secrecy in testing is that we have developed assessment in this country primarily for the allocation of opportunities. We've got to work on the issue of what education *is* in a democracy and whether the primary purpose of testing is to allocate benefits and opportunities to some and not to others, or whether the purpose of assessment to help everyone learn as much as they possibly can and become as competent as they possibly can be, so that they can make the maximum contribution to the society.

We've also had very narrow forms of assessment; if the answer is A, B, C, D, or E and if it weren't secret, you could cheat by knowing that the answer is C without that being a reflection of your own knowledge. I think that in good performance-oriented assessments, it is difficult to "cheat." If you work toward a good performance and you can indeed deliver a good performance, that means you've really learned those skills, rather than having memorized an answer which is only a superficial test of knowledge.

Pamela Moss: It is important to separate out the principles underlying a particular practice from the practice itself. For instance, one of the principles that underlie the practice of looking at items as separate pieces is that an evaluation should not be unduly influenced by the idiosyncratic perspectives of individual readers. Whatever epistemological theories one draws on, this issue of disabling biases needs to be addressed. There are, however, alternative ways of addressing the problem, admittedly some of which are less studied and understood in the educational measurement community.

Problems with "old mindsets" arise when traditional practices that have worked well in certain circumstances are viewed as the only way to serve important principles. Such mindsets narrow the possibilities for what counts as "good assessment." Here, I think that those of us within the educational measurement community who argue for alternatives can pursue some productive paths. It is most important to develop, rigorously evaluate, and make available for professional review examples of alternative practices.

Mary Diez: Norm-referenced testing may have its uses, but it has done us a disservice in central cities. Year after year, test results reinforce the notion in kids' minds, as well as in teachers' minds, that the kids can't learn.

Sometimes you do want to see what the spread of performers is, but I've seen too many kids in high school who haven't mastered basic writing or basic math. That happens when no one insists on a standard for learning.

The problem with standardized tests is that they often assume a "normal" distribution, or "Bell curve." But in teaching to standards, the goal is to make explicit what we want for every learner. For example, the

Milwaukee School Board has set, as a graduation requirement, that students will be able to argue a position using evidence. And the school system is now working to get every single student there. There will be difference, but you can get everybody there.

This is a matter of serious concern. We still want what reliability and validity stand for. We also want to assess different people in ways that aren't differentially benefiting one more than the other.

William Schafer: I think we need to expand the usual way in which we think of validity and utility, and reliability, for assessments that are instructionally oriented. Where the intent of assessment is to guide student learning and understanding, to explain the curriculum, to have students do self-diagnosis, or to have the teacher diagnose, the concepts of validity and utility, in particular, apply to the communication of the assessment.

Pamela Moss: Psychometrics brings us a number of valuable principles to guide assessment development and evaluation. These principles include the importance of supporting interpretations with multiple and diverse lines of evidence, of vigilantly seeking counter-evidence and trying out counter-interpretations to highlight problems with developing interpretations, of ensuring fair and just treatment for those who are tested, of making explicit and available for professional review the evidence and argument supporting validity conclusions, and somewhat more recently, of explicitly considering the consequences of assessment as a crucial aspect of validity research. These are, of course, principles that have analogs across different traditions of disciplined inquiry. Psychometrics also brings us a set of practices for upholding these principles—useful and productive in some circumstances, less useful and potentially constraining in others. As I suggested above, the problem comes when these practices are viewed as the only means through which important principles can be served. It is important for members of the profession to read more widely outside its disciplinary boundaries, to consider alternatives that illuminate the values and consequences of conventional choices, and to develop an ongoing stance of critical reflection with regard to its principles and practices.

9. *How do we deal with equity concerns, e.g., differential or adverse impact?*

Diana Pullin: There's been a fair amount of scrutiny of both traditional objective tests for evaluation for employment and more subjective kinds of tests for evaluation for employment.

We have two sets of legal issues. One is whether the assessment itself may be inherently biased and the other is the set of questions about whether the context in which the assessment is employed may afford evidence that the individuals were not fairly treated in the overall context in which the assessment is employed.

This is something with which we still are struggling. We know that there are certain parts of this country in which there are still courts finding new evidence that we have not yet dismantled dual school systems including very recent findings in some of the Southern states indicating that we continue to have systems of public higher education that continue to discriminate against members of minority groups. So some of the challenges have to do with whether we're affording adequate non-discriminatory educational opportunities in all systems to prepare for assessments. The other set of issues call upon us to make some very difficult judgments about the assessments themselves and the individuals serving as the reviewers. Those are a set of challenges that I'm not sure we're all ready to meet.

Lelia Vickers: I think for the first time in America, we have come to the realization that maybe one type of assessment is not adequate for all children. At the national level, we should begin to rethink whether one standard is adequate for all professionals. Even with performance assessment, sometimes the human factor comes into play and assessors may not be adequately trained to consider other variables that need to be incorporated in performance assessment.

Pamela Moss: The psychometric community has, for the most part, had a circumscribed professional response to equity concerns. While acknowledging the broader issues of social justice, the profession tends to focus its research on technical problems that raise equity concerns. "Bias" arises when there is evidence that a test is differentially valid across relevant sub-groups of examinees. Many kinds of validity evidence can point to bias, and the psychometric community works hard in its test development practices to revise tests in light of such evidence.

Clearly, tests that are judged as unbiased in a technical sense can, and do, lead to adverse impact. Here, it becomes crucial to understand the reasons for any differences observed. This involves documenting the extent to which adverse impact may be occurring, engaging in a rigorous search to understand its causes and consequences in different contexts, and using that information to improve the system. In our context, this would involve, among other things, tracing educational experiences, resources, and support that teachers have received, and working to level the playing field.

Of course, equity issues are far broader and more complex than these initial responses imply. Ultimately, they involve different perspectives, held by thoughtful people, about what constitutes good teaching and what kinds of learning are valued. Tackling the issue at this level is difficult but essential. Here, as I've suggested earlier, it is crucial to foster a multi-perspectival dialogue, not just around standards but around cases of teaching practice—particularly those cases that highlight significant issues. Proponents of different perspectives have the responsibility to provide evidence and rationale in support of their position, and, equally important, to work to understand and appreciate, to the extent possible, the argument for the alternative position. We may never reach a full national consensus—in fact, such a consensus has its own risks, not the least of which is the absence of diverse perspectives to challenge the favored approach so that its proponents remain critically reflexive—but at least it will enable us to better understand our differences. And, in working to understand our differences, we come to a better, more critical, understanding of our own perspective so that it can evolve in productive ways.

Mary Diez: We really have to make sure that people are prepared for the kinds of assessments they will be taking. That is, they need to have access to the information and knowledge required as well as appropriate practice. One evening at a Milwaukee Public School Board meeting, I testified regarding a proposal from the district's Assessment Committee to initiate portfolios for all the students in high school English. One of the board members was opposed to it because he said it wouldn't be fair if some teachers gave better assignments than others. He argued, quite rightly, that the students who didn't get good assignments would be disadvantaged by the proposal. I responded by saying, "You know, that's true *now* and we don't have any way of getting at it. This kind of performance assessment will allow the district to see where there's a need for staff development, for intervention with teachers who are not giving kids what they need."

The system does need to be clear about expectations, as well as ensure that teachers are responsible both in teaching and in assessment. We must be able to show that professional judgment is trustworthy.

William Schafer: The thing I worry about is that a more subjective assessment approach is going to increase adverse impact. I don't know that we've considered that carefully enough.

If we indeed make assessment and instruction seamless then, it seems to me, a standard exists that we have agreed is important and that students have had an opportunity to understand and achieve. Then the test, as a visible representation of the standard, becomes a vehicle for a discussion about adverse impact as part of an open process that can consider all aspects of validity evidence.

10. *What legal considerations have to be taken into account, especially as we move from older forms of assessment and psychometric principles to new approaches?*

Linda Darling-Hammond: I think we have to be very, very concerned about developing methods of assessment and methods of scoring assessments that hold up as valid and reliable, as not arbitrary, capricious, or idiosyncratic. And that's obviously an equity question as well as a legal question.

Diana Pullin: From a legal perspective, one set of questions has to do with the adequacy of preparation to succeed on the assessments. The clearest recent analogies arise in high school exit testing where the courts have held that if you're going to hold someone to a standard in a high-stakes decision like the award of a diploma, you must be able to establish as an educational institution that you have afforded the students a fair opportunity to be taught what will be covered on the test or assessment.

In a teacher education context, the same set of issues could be presented: do the assessments used to determine certification and licensure cover the skills, knowledge, and conceptual frameworks to which students have been fairly exposed in their teacher preparation program? The issue is more complex in the teacher education setting because unlike a high school setting, teacher education occurs in a context where the same state entity or related state entity that offers the certificates and licenses is often the state entity that governs the content of teacher education programs, both public and private.

Other legal issues involve concerns that tests are reliable, valid, and free from bias; that the privacy interests of examiners are protected; and that fair processes and procedures are in place to ensure that individuals are treated fairly and impartially.

Raymond Pecheone: In the past when content knowledge was measured traditionally through multiple-choice assessments, much of the legal casework focused on issues of adverse impact and disparity of scores among different populations of examinees. In the development of a standards-based system, adverse impact remains a prime concern, but in the portfolio work undertaken by INTASC, the level and kind of support a teacher receives also is a key equity concern. The burden of proof will rest with states to ensure that all candidates have equal access to support regardless of what university they may have attended or the school district in which they may be employed. The issue of support addresses the degree to which the state is obligated to put in place structures (mentorship, workshops, courses, etc.) to assist all beginning teachers in meeting new and more rigorous standards for state licensure. The issue of opportunity to learn is a legal consideration that I anticipate will have a significant impact on the design of performance-based licensure systems for teachers.

11. How does the profession best use standards and assessment to improve teaching and learning?

Pamela Moss: Clearly, the potential of standards and performance assessment to support teacher preparation and professional development depends upon how they are used and how they interact with the context in which they are used. Standards and related performance assessments are at their best when they promote and inform dialogue and evidence-based decision-making within and across the various contexts and levels of education. If used, instead, as generic prescriptions of performance, they can undermine the very reform they seek to promote.

My sense is that some policymakers have very naive theories about the relationship between the means of standards and assessment and the end of improving education. If the goal is seen simply as improving scores on the assessments, then the educational system is in trouble. There are many ways to improve scores without improving the quality of education.

Lelia Vickers: We must always try to improve the art of teaching. Standards and assessments provide a venue to focus on best practice and to reassess current best practice. Standards help the profession to critically evaluate the process of teaching. Collaboratively the faculty, along with student input, can set standards for what is expected and then share those standards with students. We set standards with contributions from those individuals who understand what good teaching is, what high standards are. As we begin to set standards, we need to show students what the expectations are, help them achieve those expectations, and give them opportunities to go back/rework/prepare again until they get to those levels of expectations.

Linda Darling-Hammond: I think that one of the most difficult things for people to understand is how to think about teaching, learning, and assessment as tightly interconnected, as always going on simultaneously, rather than assessment as something that happens at the end, primarily for giving a grade rather than for informing ongoing learning and teaching.

We all learn from feedback. The feedback has to be continuous and frequent and when it is, it's much less threatening, particularly if it's also thoughtful and constructive. When we think about the new standards that are being developed by INTASC and the National Board, for example, we might very well want to have people developing a portfolio of their work using the standards as part of what they're doing in teacher education and in ongoing professional development settings later in the career, rather than as an isolated event that comes down and kind of hits you over the head at some point in time.

12. *How can we encourage local ownership and understanding of standards? Expression in meaningful terms? Dialogue on the meaning of standards and thoughtful application of standards in the design of teaching, learning, and assessment?*

Mary Diez: We have to encourage reinvention of the wheel, over and over, so that each local effort owns its own wheel. Of course, the local wheel is going to have things in common with all the other wheels. That's why I encourage institutions not to take the INTASC standards word for word but to create their own vision of the kinds of teachers they're preparing and then to use the INTASC standards as a kind of foil against which to examine their own expression for gaps or special insights.

It has to happen at the local level. But the national standards in mathematics, for instance, have really helped us focus at all levels about what good mathematics teaching is. Applying these standards at the local level across the country has led to a really strong consensus.

Linda Darling-Hammond: People need to have the opportunity to try teaching standards on: to try them out and use them in a variety of ways for a variety of purposes and make them their own. They need to find ways to knit them into their daily work and decision-making. In the case of teaching standards, I would hope we would begin to see, for example, teachers using National Board standards as a basis by which to build teacher evaluation and professional development systems rather than the standards sort of sitting off somewhere in a national office.

Diana Pullin: We know enough about failed education reform initiatives to know that unless the individuals involved in the endeavor really take these goals to heart and act on them locally, the initiative will fail. I may be being a little optimistic here, but I think that there is more of a shared understanding among those who stay up-to-date with the literature and the research development. There should be some shared core understanding about what is good teaching and how to assess it that we could agree is a norm across our institutions, but one that would also allow for some individual variations so that we might focus in one place on a particular theme and you might focus on another. We could still prepare what we would agree would be equally good teachers.

Pamela Moss: The vision of teaching fostered by standards like those of INTASC and the National Board requires time for professional development—not just the time involved in teacher education or even regular inservice programs, but time to collaborate with one's colleagues. To assume that teachers are doing their jobs only when they are engaged in active contact with students is seriously counterproductive. We need to help educational policymakers, administrators, and the public to understand the crucial importance of time for collaborative professional development, instructional planning, and reflection on what has occurred.

13. How can we promote ongoing assessment that contributes to reflective practice?

Raymond Pecheone: We can approach this by designing assessments that invite teachers to be reflective about aspects of their work that are grounded in the standards, as well as in what they do on the job. Teacher reflection should not happen in isolation but should be embedded in a process that promotes collaboration and cooperation among teachers. The INTASC portfolio project is an example of how an assessment and support system can be built around the importance of teacher reflection. The adaptations that teachers cite as a result of reflecting on their practice are a significant component of the INTASC scoring process. If you design an assessment system that ignores the importance of teacher thinking, especially with high-stakes assessments, the likelihood of institutions paying attention to reflective practice is significantly diminished.

Diana Pullin: We should not ask of others anything more than we ask of ourselves. Unless those of us in institutions of higher education are willing to engage in our critical self-reflection and difficult discourse over these issues, I don't think we can hold others accountable for similar kinds of initiatives. That will be quite a challenge for all of us in higher education.

We have to begin from the earliest stages of teacher preparation to create a context and a professional culture in which we have not only these acts of self-reflection and this continuous process of professional development, but in which we also have tough-minded and fair—and open—evaluative discussions about the quality of our work.

Pamela Moss: Periodic milestones, like those provided by teacher education institutions, states, NCATE, INTASC, and NBPTS, provide irregular formal opportunities for assessment. And, undoubtedly, they promote some ongoing reflection as teachers prepare for these milestones. However, they are not sufficient to encourage the kind of evidence-based critical reflection that sustains one throughout a career.

While we can all work to promote such opportunities in our own local contexts, it is important that those who set policy provide the necessary time, incentives, and partnerships to foster this kind of professional practice. It is also crucial that such dialogues occur in an atmosphere of trust where teachers can ask for and offer supportive critical commentary without fear of reprisal or embarrassment. Here, it is important for those in authority to distinguish those high-stakes moments where consequential career decisions are made from ongoing assessment and support.

How to build a culture where there is sufficient trust to sustain shared critical reflection is not an easy question to address, although there are existence proofs which might be studied. In contexts where shared critical reflection has not been part of daily practice, it will take some courageous first steps by colleagues who are willing to "open their classroom doors," reflect more publicly on their work, and invite critical commentary. As Diana has suggested, we would do well to begin with our own educational institutions—not just by encouraging shared critical reflection among those we teach or otherwise support, but by engaging in and inviting it ourselves.

Mary Diez: The critical part is using assessment information to surprise ourselves—to be able to see something, because we're looking at it from the assessment angle, that we wouldn't have seen otherwise.

14. *What policies are likely to promote the development of the profession as well as make players at the various levels accountable and responsible?*

Raymond Pecheone: What is needed is a comprehensive policy structure that addresses the full range of teachers' experience throughout their careers. Standards for preparation, induction, and advanced certification need to be formulated and connected across the teaching continuum. Operationally, this means that state licensure will move from a system that relies on bureaucratic structures and course-counting as the primary means of licensure to a system that is both standards- and outcomes-based. In addition, states would institute policies whereby standards and assessment for teachers as well as those for students would be aligned and compatible. Moreover, professional development and teacher evaluation would be directly linked to standards for students and teachers to foster a coherent and systematic process of support for all teachers.

Linda Darling-Hammond's commission report, *What Matters Most: Teaching For America's Future*, provides a good blueprint that states can follow to institute policies that will promote the development of the profession while at the same time assisting in putting in place standards of accountability that promote teaching and learning. INTASC is following many of these polices in the development of its work.

Linda Darling-Hammond: There were several important policies endorsed in the report of the National Commission. One is the creation of a professional standards board like those that other professions have long had. This is the governance mechanism by which professions can develop, continue to refine and revise, enforce, and transmit standards. Standards boards are important because you need continually to tend and nurture the standards, to use them and revise them.

Another is the move to ensure that all schools of education are eventually professionally accredited and are able to look through the lenses of professional standards at their own program-building efforts.

Another is performance-based licensing policies that incorporate the kinds of standards and assessments INTASC has been developing. Such systems would ensure that everyone who was admitted to teaching has met common standards and can use certain kinds of knowledge and skills on behalf of the kids.

Finally, I think we need policies that support teachers in pursuing ongoing professional development that is aimed at the development of their practice in relation to professional standards like the National Board certification process. Teachers ought to be acknowledged and recognized in some way for having achieved certification, whether it's a salary stipend or whether it's their recognition as teacher education colleagues, as mentors and cooperating teachers, or as participants in other roles and activities which recognize their expertise and dedication.

Lelia Vickers: I would like to see in policy a series of alternative ways of granting initial licensure that are grounded in research and theory, from which we then get another way to assess performance. I would like to see the state make policies that allow us teacher educators to develop a "pluralistic" approach to assessment.

If we are going to have professional teachers model effective behaviors, to set high expectations for all students, we have to begin in the preparation program to say, "All individuals do not learn in the same way." If we want them to reach their potential, we must employ strategies that use the modalities through which they learn; otherwise, I don't think we'll ever be successful in providing all children equal opportunities to high-quality education.

Some policymakers recommend policies that they know little about. The profession must come together and begin to make recommendations that are grounded in the research and current best practice. That procedure would support optimal learning for all children.

Diana Pullin: The evidence from some of the recent literature on P–12 education reform indicates that there is more likelihood of success if you take a systemic approach to a reform initiative. Part of what I think we have to be careful to assess as we go about implementing these changes is whether or not we are being systemic and systematic in our own efforts to enhance teacher preparation.

As a matter of policy, we need to be working collaboratively with our colleagues in the other units on campus who assist in the education of future teachers. Policy must assure collaboration between institutions of higher education and the state entities that regulate teacher education and the various state agencies that will be making the certification or licensure decision.

Mary Diez: It's a very difficult thing to create a policy that will make good things happen and not prevent good things from happening. There's a danger that unanticipated consequences will undo the good intent of policy.

15. *What states are examples of effective reform in progress?*

Raymond Pecheone: Much reform in the states has emanated from the seminal work of Lee Shulman, and Stanford University's Teacher Assessment Project (TAP). Connecticut and California began a partnership in the 1980s that attempted to model the work of the TAP program in these two states. The collaboration of the two states resulted in the founding of INTASC. Currently, through INTASC, 37 states are involved in reforming their teacher assessment and licensure systems. Ten states have pooled resources to begin the development of standards-based portfolio systems for the induction and licensure of new teachers.

In addition, 27 states are working on a performance test of teacher professional knowledge that will be used for the initial licensure of beginning teachers. My home state of Connecticut started early in the support and assessment process and was the first state to put standards-based portfolio systems operationally online in fiscal year 1996-97. Currently, portfolios are required in the areas of mathematics, English/language arts, science, and special education. By the year 2000, portfolios will be required in the following areas: social studies, art, music, elementary education, physical education, and administration. These ten licensure areas represent 90 percent of the teacher and administrator licenses granted in Connecticut. The Connecticut program is a two-year program of support and assessment for teachers to be eligible for a professional license. All beginning teachers in Connecticut receive support through a statewide mentoring program. In addition, the state sponsors clinics, workshops, seminars, and college courses that are directly linked to teacher standards and are available to both mentors and beginning teachers.

Other endeavors worthy of note are Indiana's projects on standards and development; Kentucky and Rhode Island's efforts in preservice assessment and support; and the New York, Connecticut, and California programs in the design of observational systems to evaluate teachers.

Linda Darling-Hammond: I think Connecticut is a good example of reform in progress. They've probably been at it longer than anyone else. In 1986, they boosted and equalized spending for beginning teacher salaries while they also raised licensing standards at the same time. In recent years, they have put online the set of portfolio performance assessments for beginning teachers that are the model for the INTASC portfolio process. The reforms in Connecticut have eliminated teacher shortages while increasing teachers' knowledge and skills and improving education for children.

Many other states have launched similar reforms more recently. Indiana's professional standards board has created a set of plans to put NCATE, INTASC, and National Board standards in place, thus creating the continuum that will support teacher learning at various points in their careers. Ohio is pursuing a very similar strategy. North Carolina is about to pursue such a strategy with its new legislation that has created a standards board and charged it with a series of reforms to improve teacher education, licensing, and professional development. Illinois is in the beginning steps of doing something very similar. So there are a lot of places around the country that are working on this agenda. The National Commission on Teaching & America's Future has 12 partner states that have agreed to work together to implement the commission's recommendations, which include recommendations to create this continuum of teaching standards, new assessments, and opportunities for teacher learning.

Mary Diez: In Kentucky, the intent is to put in place performance assessments for licensure based on samples being developed and piloted in schools of education. In Wisconsin, the current administrative code for teacher education remains operative while institutions build the capacity for more performance-based programs. Both of those are common-sense approaches to policy.

16. What is the impact of NCATE/State Partnerships and the New Professional Teacher project?

Linda Darling-Hammond: The New Professional Teacher project is basically trying to launch conversations among key stakeholders within states to focus on what teachers need to know and be able to do and how policies can be created to support that.

In just a few years, NCATE has moved from having very little opportunity to work productively with states to having partnerships with more than 40 states. These partnerships are allowing states to figure out how to use NCATE standards in the review process for schools of education. Over time, I hope that becomes a process by which state boards of education and professional standards boards use professional accreditation as the basis for approving programs and put their energy into developing meaningful licensing systems.

Diana Pullin: The impact can be quite salutary if we all participate in this dialogue and we use it as a meaningful opportunity to reflect on what we're doing. It's an opportunity, though, in which we have to have the tough-minded discussion without losing sight of the need to be collaborative and coordinated. It's the same kind of call for challenging behavior that we're asking of our teacher education candidates.

17. What can we learn from the "partner states" formed to follow up on the National Commission report?

Mary Diez: I disagree with the assertion of the National Commission and the Holmes Group that teacher education ought to be conducted in a specific type of PDS structure, with a five- or six-year program. I think we need to be clear about our purpose in preparing teachers and have the structure match the purpose. We should not start with the structure as a guide to policy. I think it's still possible—and in fact our program at Alverno is an existence proof—to produce good teachers in a four-year baccalaureate program. It may be that not a lot of institutions can do that because of other issues, but policy should not preclude the possibility.

Pamela Moss: Given what my colleagues have said, I'll simply highlight the importance of engaging in ongoing research that makes explicit the consequences of different policy choices. Here, we need to encourage those responsible to engage in or otherwise support multi-perspectival studies, including both case studies and larger-scale investigations, that trace the outcomes (intended and unintended) of policies as they are implemented. Those of us who set or inform policy should expect of ourselves no less than we expect of the teachers whose lives we impact: consideration of complex evidence, collaborative inquiry, and critical reflection on our own theories and practices.

18. *What information should states expect teacher preparation programs to provide about how their programs prepare teachers?*

Linda Darling-Hammond: The school of education ought to be able to say, "Here is how we ensure, for example, that teachers know about learning theory. Here is how we make sure that they know about developing skills in identifying and addressing the needs of diverse learners, whether that diversity is a function of students' approaches to learning, special needs of the students, a different language background, or a different cultural and community background." Schools of education ought to be able to show how they're preparing students to develop particular abilities in a way that is credible and defensible. I think accreditors ought to be looking at (teacher education) students' work, their portfolios, their performances of various kinds. They ought to be able to see what the outcome of the educational process is. They also need to be concerned about what students know when they begin the process and what the developmental contribution has been of the school of education. They should care about the diversity of the student body and the extent to which the school has made a commitment to preparing teachers of all racial and ethnic backgrounds for a variety of kinds of teaching situations. I think it would be a mistake for us to repeat what some Southern states did in the 1980s, which was to begin to make approval decisions for schools of education solely on the basis of past scores on licensing exams. What that did was create an incentive for schools of education to essentially pre-screen out candidates who couldn't already pass the exit exam, rather than to improve the quality of their own programs. I don't think we want to replicate that mistake.

Pamela Moss: I think it is crucial that teacher preparation programs hold themselves accountable for the quality of the decisions they make. This means that there should be ongoing evidence-based program review, open to the scrutiny of responsible others, that considers both the quality of the program and the validity of its recommendations.

Raymond Pecheone: Higher education has to be a partner so that— with respect to the standards that we adopt, the accountability systems that we use, the licensure process that we use for new teachers—all of those work in combination and in partnership with higher education.

PART II

Using Standards & Assessment to Reform Teacher Education: Seven Examples

Introduction

■

Mary E. Diez

This section comprises nine essays reflecting the stories of seven institutions which have approached the reform of teacher education through attention to standards and assessment.

Six of the essays represent institutions that were involved in the *Teaching for Tomorrow* Project. Faculty from Alverno College, Clayton College & State University, the University of Northern Colorado, and Winston-Salem State University describe a common set of key activities, following the goals of the project itself—i.e., each clarified the outcomes of its programs, made changes to develop a more coherent curriculum, developed performance assessment processes both to develop and to document the development of student learning outcomes, and developed strategies to involve faculty across the institution and P–12 schools in the reform effort. In addition, each essay reflects specific aspects of institutional context that guided how the four goal areas were addressed by the *Teaching for Tomorrow* Project institutions.

The remaining three essays describe institutions which, while not part of the *Teaching for Tomorrow* Project, engaged in some of the same key activities. For example, reflecting Kentucky's reform goals, Asbury College's Lowe and Banker target assessment in their essay. The description of Ashland University's reform efforts written by Schnug and Shelly puts the primary focus on the process of clarifying outcomes. And Central Missouri State's Mihalevich and Carr highlight how faculty interest in continuous process improvement and constructivism sparked work in performance assessment.

Guiding Coherence: Performance-Based Teacher Education at Alverno College

■

Mary E. Diez, Jacqueline M. Hass, Kathryn Henn-Reinke,
Julie A. Stoffels, and Leona C. Truchan

The context for changes in teacher education programs at Alverno College can be understood best in relationship to changes in the college's definition of liberal education. This definition focuses on the student's abilities that are promoted by the teaching/learning exchange between faculty and students and by the assessment of the student's development of those abilities.

Alverno faculty undertook the development of a performance-based baccalaureate degree over 20 years ago (Alverno College Faculty, 1994; Diez, 1994; Loacker, Cromwell, & O'Brien, 1986), but the questions that they faced in redesigning the undergraduate curriculum and the liberal arts and professional majors continue to be current. What does it mean to say a student has completed a liberal arts baccalaureate degree? What does it mean that she has completed the requirements of a biology, English, mathematics, or social science major in a professional program in secondary education? How does the curriculum provide a coherent and developmental support to her learning? What counts as evidence that a student has achieved the expectations of the degree, the major, and the professional preparation?

A major learning of the Alverno faculty over the past 20 years is that performance assessment is not an add-on to business as usual. Focusing on what students can do with what they know *transforms* both the curriculum and approaches to teaching. A well-defined assessment plan in the teacher education program provides opportunities to see the consistency of development as it is demonstrated through multiple modes of assessment and in multiple contexts. In addition, assessment enhances learning by providing many opportunities for the development of self-assessment as well as ongoing feedback to a student on her development as a professional. In a program conceived of merely as a collection of courses, the whole is the sum of its parts and the parts can be delivered and received as separate entities. In a program conceived of as the development of learners' abilities, the equation is changed. The parts begin to be seen as interrelated and interdependent; moreover, each part (learning outcomes, learning experiences, and assessments, as well as courses) becomes open to examination in relationship to the performance of learners.

Throughout our work with other teacher educators across the country, especially in relationship to reconceptualizing programs to meet NCATE standards and state standards, Alverno teacher education faculty have found three elements useful as a framework for moving toward a performance-based teacher education program: clarity of outcomes, the design of learning experiences, and the design of performance assessment. We also have found that the ultimate success of reform efforts hinges on a university-wide commitment as well as on involvement of P–12 practitioners throughout the process.

Clarity of Outcomes

Essential to the development of a performance-based teacher education program is its reconceptualization in terms of what teachers need to know and be able to do. For teacher educators who may think about a program in terms of a collection of courses rather than in terms of learning outcomes achieved by students, this is a major shift.

Even though teacher educators can draw upon a range of teacher education outcomes and standards available to them in the literature, we believe that it is important for the faculty of each program to think through the conceptualization of the abilities of the teacher in their own words. To those who say, "Don't reinvent the wheel," we argue that you *do* need to find your own way to reinvent the wheel if you are to *own* the wheel.

The Alverno outcomes, for example, were developed by a group of faculty in the late 1970s (Diez, 1990). While these outcomes have been revised both out of our experience of working with them and as we reviewed emerging national standards in relationship to them, they remain a useful description of the knowledge, skills, and dispositions of the teacher:

1. Conceptualization: Integrating content knowledge with educational frameworks and a broadly based understanding of the liberal arts to plan and implement instruction.
2. Diagnosis: Relating observed behavior to relevant frameworks in order to determine and implement learning prescriptions.
3. Coordination: Managing resources effectively to support learning goals.
4. Communication: Using verbal, nonverbal, and media modes of communication to establish the environment of the classroom and to structure and reinforce learning.
5. Integrative Interaction: Acting with professional values as a situational decision-maker, adapting to the changing needs of the environment to develop students as learners.

Each education outcome ability is described for faculty and candidates in "maps" (see Table 1 for an example of one of the five maps—Integrative Interaction). These maps also define the teacher's ongoing professional growth, moving from a description of what is expected when the teacher is licensed and first employed, to what is expected when she has gained some classroom experience, to what is expected when she becomes a master teacher. For example, the model of ongoing teacher development in the ability on integrative interaction describes the beginning teacher as "showing respect for varied learner perspectives," the experienced teacher as "providing structures within which learners create their own perspectives," and the master teacher as "assisting learners in the habit of taking multiple perspectives."

As is evident in Table 1, we believe it important to capture the interaction between knowing and doing in the statement of the outcomes. Many teacher educators have found it difficult to move beyond a description of specific knowledge in conceptualizing outcomes. To help break out of the "knowledge box," we suggest using these questions: What would the teacher *do* with that knowledge? *Why* is that knowledge essential to the teacher's practice?

Design of Learning Experiences

The outcomes are just the beginning. Once conceptualized, teacher educators need to use the outcomes to guide the design of learning expe-

Table 1.

INTEGRATIVE INTERACTION
Demonstrating Professional Responsibility in Diverse Learning Environments

Expectations for the Beginning Teacher	Expectations for the Developing Teacher	Expectations for the Experienced Professional Teacher
Believing as a *director* of learning in the developing knowledge, understanding and abilities of learners	Believing as a *colleague* with learners in sharing responsibility for learning	Believing as an *advocate* of learning in motivating, in relating to the learner, in sharing judgment
Perceiving and responding to basic elements of the complex of variables present in interaction, e.g., roles, developmental levels, situation, relational definitions, emotions, content, environment, etc. • Welcoming and celebrating diversity • Listening/connecting/providing different perspectives in response to learner activity • Giving satisfactory answers to learner's questions/comments • Stimulating learners to question and respond • Guiding interlearner discussion • Modeling learning by making explicit what one is doing • Encouraging individual participation while effectively directing group activity • Using feedback to assist learners to become self-starting learners • Nurturing learner development	Demonstrating growing awareness of the complex of variables present in interaction • Recognizing how aspects of interaction affect the teacher and the teacher's strategies • Adapting possible responses out of increased experience • Enlarging one's repertoire of interaction skills • Differentiating responses in interacting one-on-one and with the group	Demonstrating sophisticated awareness of the complex of variables present in interaction, their mutual impact, and their ongoing negotiation by the interactants • Constantly making adjustments in activities, not out of a pre-planned program, but in response to relevance of learners' experience and knowledge and the reality of the broader societal sphere of influence on their lives • Using nonverbal cues to test out ways in which the responsibility/activity for learning can be shifted to the learner

Demonstrating awareness of the limitations inherent in the situation, the learners, and self
• Showing respect for varied learner perspectives
• Demonstrating an adequate understanding of individual differences, especially cultural, gender and psychological differences
• Dealing with individuals in a way that recognizes their personal qualities
• Making connections between/among different cultural groups
• Designing learning to best relate to the characteristics of the group and individuals within it
• Reflecting an awareness of the effect of media on learning
• Taking responsibility
  for diagnosis and assessment (and sharing both with learner)
  for intervention by designing effective strategies for growth
• Dealing with a range of classroom situations with confidence and calm
	Extending ability to assist learners to become more independent
	• Providing structures within which learners can create their own perspectives
	• Providing other perspectives for learners to test their knowledge
	• Providing a wide range of media and technology options to engage learners with multiple perspectives and global issues
		Assisting learners in the habit of taking multiple perspectives
		• Showing commitment to the process of going from experience to conceptualization
		• Encouraging learners to seek out and explore multiple perspectives

	Taking responsibility for increasing professionalism • Developing identification as a professional • Acting on professional values • Relating effectively with peers and superiors • Relating to systems and institutions • Seeking opportunities to develop new skills/knowledge	Taking responsibility for and to the state of education • Identifying as a professional • Acting out of an explicit philosophy of education • Working with local/broader spheres of influence • Promoting others to become technology supporters • Advocating for the use of technology in education • Facilitating curriculum reform through the integration of media and technology

Diez, Hass, Henn-Reinke, Stoffels, & Truchan

riences—both in courses and in field experiences. When Alverno education faculty began the redesign process in the 1980s, we projected what kinds of learning experiences are needed to develop the abilities (knowledge, skills, and dispositions) described by the outcomes. Then, faculty members inventoried the kinds of learning experiences already incorporated in the program, revealing both gaps and redundancies and raising faculty awareness of the curriculum as a whole.

We worked to build a coherent, developmental curriculum—making the parts integrally connected and mutually reinforcing. Our experience is that interaction skills need to be nurtured over time and linked to growing conceptual skills if candidates are to be able to design learning to best relate to the characteristics of the group and the learners within it, as specified in the map of the integrative interaction ability (Table 1).

Focusing on student development of the outcome abilities has made our faculty more aware of what learning experiences are most useful and which are less so. Looking across courses and experiences has kept the curriculum open to larger revisions, sparked by external demands (like the urban school's increasingly diverse student population) or internal review (e.g., a critical look at the performance of graduates). Thus, developing such a curriculum requires continuous, recursive work.

Design of Performance Assessment

If outcomes for the program are stated as abilities—i.e., complex combinations of knowledge, skills, values, attitudes, and dispositions—then assessment processes need to elicit complex evidence in student performance (Alverno College Faculty, 1994). Basic skills may be able to be tested by a fairly narrow measure or set of measures. For refined and extended expectations, and because of the developmental nature of the behaviors, the kind of complex evidence required demands multiple opportunities for candidates to demonstrate their growing abilities, using a variety of assessment modes.

Our work is grounded in Alverno's pioneering efforts in performance assessment across the undergraduate curriculum for the past 20 years (Alverno College Faculty, 1994). With our colleagues in liberal arts and the other professional areas, we see assessment serving both to document the development of the abilities and to contribute to candidate development. When our candidates *practice* the abilities that will be demanded of them as teachers, and when we use assessment and feedback to help them *develop* those abilities further, assessment is a powerful guide to growth. In this way, assessment becomes integral to learning.

The Alverno faculty's development of "assessment-as-learning" underscores the importance of assessment in guiding student growth. This term describes

> a multidimensional process, integral to learning, that involves observing performance of an individual learner in action and judging them on the basis of public, developmental criteria, with resulting feedback to the learner. (Alverno College Faculty, 1994)

The Alverno faculty's use of the term "assessment-as-learning" is intended to highlight the importance of the process for candidates and distinguish it from institutional and program assessment. Essential to our concept and practice of assessment-as-learning are these characteristics:

1. Expected learning outcomes or abilities. With a focus on the development of the five education outcome abilities, candidates are aware of the goals toward which they are working. Alverno faculty believe that making the conceptual frameworks of the program explicit makes learning more available to students. In each course syllabus, the five abilities are integrated with specific course content in the design of course goals. For example, in early field experience placements in classroom settings, candidates know that they are expected to "encourage individual participation while effectively directing group activities" and "show respect for varied learner perspectives" as goals focused on integrative interaction.

2. Explicit criteria for performance. The translation of the expected outcomes into specific criteria that provide a more complete description of what the outcome might look like in practice is a difficult but essential process. What elements of a performance are most critical? How good is good enough? How can "good" be described without precluding multiple approaches to achieving it?

Candidates can use criteria to guide their work and to provide a structure for self-assessment. In an assessment developed at Alverno, teacher education candidates enrolled in their third field experience participate in an external assessment of professional group interaction. In this assessment, they prepare for a simulated meeting of teachers in an urban school district who are working with the district's mission statement, examining it in relationship to current issues in education (e.g., inclusion, race and ethnicity, integrated curriculum, etc.). Each candidate prepares in advance for a meeting in which she will take the role of teacher by reading a common article and analyzing the mission statement's underlying assumptions in relationship to her own beliefs about education and in terms of the focus area she has been assigned. In the group discussion, she is expected to represent her own views as well as to respond on the spot to the positions of others. Candidates need to show that they can advocate for a position, while also respecting those who may hold different, even conflicting, positions.

Criteria for this assessment address both the manner of interaction expected in professional settings and the quality of thought brought to bear on the issues in the discussion. For example, assessors look to see how each candidate evokes the ideas of others through questioning, demonstrates flexibility in discussing opposing ideas, and articulates the impact of potential decisions on others in the organization.

Because we are aware that abilities develop over time and that candidates need multiple opportunities to both practice and demonstrate these abilities, many experiences, incorporated across the curriculum, are designed to give them practice and assist them to reflect on their growth. For example, one criterion above addresses the ability of candidates to demonstrate flexibility in discussing opposing ideas. In the three-course, integrated reading curriculum, candidates explore varied approaches to reading and language arts and articulate the major arguments in favor of each. In addition, they demonstrate their ability to advocate for a particular position using reasoned judgment.

Criteria may be developed or adapted collaboratively by candidates and faculty for use in specific courses, building upon our common understanding of the meaning of integrative interaction and the other education outcome abilities. Criteria are discussed with candidates before the assessment, reviewed by candidates as they prepare for the assessment, and used again as candidates self-assess their completed performance.

3. Expert judgment. Alverno faculty members assess a candidate's performance thoughtfully. They gather evidence from the candidate's performance and weigh it against the criteria they have developed. For example, in the professional group interaction assessment described above, faculty reviewing both the written materials and the videotaped discussion of a group of four or five candidates will note areas of strength—e.g., that all of the candidates articulated their ideas clearly, drawing upon their resources as well as their analysis of the mission statement itself. They will also use evidence to identify weaknesses and make suggestions for development. For example, some candidates who are well-prepared for presenting their own view may find it difficult to revise their view in the light of new evidence. They may, in fact, fail to demonstrate respect for other perspectives, as evidenced in their lack of nonverbal attention to another's speaking or explicit rejection of another's ideas.

4. Productive feedback. In reviewing student performance, the faculty member's work is not aimed at judgment alone, but on the ongoing development of the student. Her careful examination of the candidate's overall performance as well as specific examples within it provides the basis for feedback. She provides links between her judgment and the evidence—both the candidate's written work (analytical preparation worksheets and post-taping reflection) and the videotape of the discussion. Feedback, keyed to the criteria for a quality performance, is given in various modes—sometimes oral, sometimes written, sometimes individually, and sometimes in a group. Often, peer feedback is incorporated into the process, assisting candidates to learn the meaning of the criteria by having the experience of examining another's performance and finding evidence of strengths and weaknesses therein.

5. Self-assessment. Throughout the program, Alverno faculty have designed all assessments to include the experience of reflective self-assessment. The program's success in helping candidates develop abilities of reflective practice hinges on performance assessments that not only elicit the habits of mind and the skills of the reflective practitioner, but also clearly frame what candidates need to reflect upon. Because performance assessments are situated in authentic contexts and teaching roles, with criteria specifying the expected level of performance, candidates can more easily focus on specific ways they need to improve their teaching than if they merely learned *about* reflective practice. Moreover, in coming to see assessment as integral, they overcome whatever tendencies toward defensiveness they may have demonstrated at the beginning of their studies. Most important, developing skill in self-assessment prepares candidates to make habitual the disposition to examine and refine their practice so that, when they leave the supportive environment of their teacher preparation program, they are ready to work as autonomous practitioners.

6. Assessment as a process involving multiple performances. Alverno teacher education candidates will experience hundreds of assessments in their undergraduate program. Rather than seeing assessment as separated from learning, they come to see it as a part of learning. Rather than seeing any one assessment as the "whole story," they recognize that any assessment is a *sample* of performance. The cumulative picture that they draw through experiencing assessment-as-learning across their courses provides an ever deeper and richer portrait of themselves as teachers-to-be. Likewise, assessment in multiple modes, methods, and times provides the faculty with confidence in their judgment of the candidate's development of the abilities of a teacher.

Alverno faculty believe that performance assessments are most beneficial when they come as close as possible to the realistic experiences of the practicing teacher. In developing the curriculum for teacher education, they have identified a number of roles that teachers play, including but going beyond the primary role of facilitator of learning in the classroom. Therefore, performance assessments of the abilities of a teacher may be simulated to focus on parent-teacher interaction, multidisciplinary team evaluation, the teacher's work with district or building planning, or the teacher's citizenship role, as well as on actual classroom teaching performance in the field experience and student teaching classrooms. In this way, performance assessments provide candidates with successive approximations of the role of the teacher.

In advanced courses, students focus not only on the education abilities, but also on the varied contexts for their application. Student teaching, of course, provides a laboratory in which to practice the key elements of integrative interaction, which addresses both the dispositions and philosophical positions guiding interaction with others and the quality of the interaction itself. Candidates gather evidence from their work across time in student teaching, drawing upon videotapes, live observations by their cooperating teacher and college supervisor, lesson plans, student responses, and ongoing reflective journals. A set of descriptors guides the candidate's self-assessment as well as the judgment process of the cooperating teacher and supervisor. For example, candidates need to demonstrate their integrative interaction in areas like the following:
- Shows rapport with students
- Shows respect for varied student perspectives
- Stimulates students to question and respond
- Guides interstudent discussion
- Guides pace of learning activities
- Deals with a range of classroom situations with confidence and calm
- Shows ability to make decisions and to take responsibility for them
- Assesses own performance
  - gaining a sense of the interaction of the group as affecting learning
  - recognizing students' personal backgrounds and reading their non-verbal communication to respond appropriately

Conclusion

As is clear from these examples, the change in the teacher education programs at Alverno College puts assessment at the heart of the teaching and learning process. For us, the power of assessment-as-learning is in the ongoing interaction between teacher and learner, focused on the learner's continuous development. Far from being an add-on, assessment is grounded in our conceptualization of the abilities of the teacher and is integrally linked to learning experiences in classes and fieldwork.

■

References

Alverno College Faculty. (1994). *Student assessment-as-learning at Alverno College.* Milwaukee, WI: Alverno Productions.

Diez, M. (1990). A thrust from within: Reconceptualizing teacher education at Alverno College. *Peabody Journal of Education, 65*(2), 4-18.

Diez, M. (1994). Probing the meaning of assessment. In *Essays on emerging assessment issues* (pp. 5-11). Washington, DC: American Association of Colleges for Teacher Education.

Diez, M. & Hass, J. (in press). No more piecemeal reform: Using performance-based approaches to rethink teacher education. *Action in Teacher Education.*

Loacker, G., Cromwell, L., & O'Brien, K. (1986). Assessment in higher education: To serve the learner. In C. Adelman (Ed.), *Assessment in higher education: Issues and contexts* (Report No. OR 86-301, pp. 47-62). Washington, DC: U.S. Department of Education.

Preparing Teachers at Asbury College: Restructuring for the 21st Century

■

Verna J. Lowe and Bonnie J. Banker

The landmark decision that declared Kentucky's system of education unconstitutional resulted in the 1990 Kentucky Education Reform Act (KERA) mandating systemic reform throughout the commonwealth. From the initial response to the reform effort, Kentucky educators committed to a performance-based accountability system of teacher preparation. Coupled with performance assurance was a commitment to P–12 collaboration resulting in authentic training. With Kentucky's approach to redefined preparation culminating in accountability, training institutions were challenged to restructure preparation programs that were multifaceted and dynamic in program design to assure quality performance and authenticity.

Professional Standards

As Kentucky engages in systemic educational reform, institutions of higher education realize the process of training teachers must radically change adequately to prepare teachers to implement the reform efforts. A significant feature of moving from a traditional program to a performance-based accountability system is the adoption of professional standards that embody the outcomes for teacher preparation in Kentucky. From the outset, Kentucky's commitment was to the development of performance indicators with accompanying criteria that reflect the essence of a teacher prepared to teach in the 21st century. In spring 1994, the New Teacher Standards (NTS) were adopted as regulation for teacher preparation throughout Kentucky. As the NTS were being formally adopted, the Interstate New Teacher Assessment and Support Consortium (INTASC) was involved in developing standards to be used at the national level. Interestingly, a strong correlation is clearly identified between the NTS and INTASC standards. The strength and value of these standards are in the guidance provided through prescribed outcomes for performance-based preparation and assessment.

Asbury College accepted the challenge of program restructuring and sought to craft a performance-based teacher preparation program designed to train educators for the cutting edge of educational renewal. We found the total restructuring of our program involved five phases:

- conceptualization
- development
- integration
- evaluation
- refinement

In Table 1, we outline the activities and products within each of the phases that have resulted from our restructuring process. Our conceptualizing phase of restructuring began in spring 1993, and we have progressed through the phases and find ourselves at the point of refinement. Evaluation and refinement are naturally linked as one informs the other. Refinement is at the heart of the restructuring process to maintain a dynamic preparation system.

Within the past three years, our training program has been redesigned to include:

- the adoption of Kentucky's New Teacher Standards as a guide to measure professional competency;
- the integration of a constructivist conceptual framework throughout the preparation program;
- the design and full implementation of an award-winning Continuous Assessment Model;
- the preparation and implementation of professional portfolios;
- the redesign of the curriculum to meet Kentucky's streamlined certification;
- the active involvement of our content faculty in the curricular redesign and the delivery of the Continuous Assessment process;
- the integral inclusion of P–12 professionals in training and evaluating preprofessionals; and

Table 1. Phases of a Restructured Teacher Preparation Program

PHASES OF RESTRUCTURING	ACTIVITIES	PRODUCTS
Conceptualization	Collaborate on aligning program to institutional mission	Department mission statement
	Design conceptual framework based on the constructivist philosophy	Document including theme, schematic, framework model, and supporting research
Development	Create a process for continuous assessment of the NTS	Continuous Assessment Model
	Design authentic assessment package	On-demand performance tasks; portfolio process; integrated field-based experiences; required community service
	Redesign curriculum to accommodate performance-based measures	Curriculum folios
	Enhance P-12 collaboration	Collaborative grant; P-12 mentors--vital role in field experiences; P-12 team members in interviews & portfolio reviews for continuous assessment process; Kentucky Teacher Internship Program
Integration	Embed conceptual framework into the delivery system, resulting in a spiral curriculum	Redesigned course syllabi; integrated portfolio requirements; authentic instructional techniques; restructured curriculum
	Implement New Teacher Standards across program and within courses	Course objectives matched to NTS within courses and program folios; portfolio framework
	Collaborate within and across disciplines	Curriculum workshops; department consultations
	Apply Continuous Assessment Model across program and within courses	Performance assessment checkpoints (Gates 1-4); multiple measures within courses and applied across the program
Evaluation	Generate formative and summative data on students, curriculum, and program	Data from portfolio assessment by NTS criteria; structured interview response; on-demand performance tasks; student self-assessment; faculty recommendations; P-12 mentors' evaluation; mastery of course competencies; NTE or PRAXIS results
	Biannual program review	Data from NTE or PRAXIS results; validation from external P-12 panel; biannual department reviews; dissemination of NTE or PRAXIS results to programs; alumni survey
Refinement	Systematic revisiting of evaluative data	Department meetings
	Involve department in state and national issues	Professional presentations and publications
	Revise models based on practice	Redesigned portfolio rubrics/structured interview questions; handbook revision

- the development and implementation of authentic tasks for assessment purposes.

The result of this restructuring of our program is a new kind of preservice educator whose performance reflects a holistic training program. Our preservice educators embody the true essence of a professional teacher because of the rigor of our program, a focus on authenticity, and the systematic feedback of student progress through our Continuous Assessment Model. As we aggressively address reform, our training program at Asbury College serves as a frame of reference for other institutions within the state.

Continuous Assessment Model

Our reform efforts launched the development of a conceptual framework incorporating a facilitative, constructivist teacher preparation model as its theme. With an intentional curriculum design and pervasive facilitative model, the focus of the Education Department is to produce educators who can support and facilitate student success. Our conceptual framework is embedded throughout the curriculum and has an impact on our performance assessment. As we seek to guide our students in being facilitators of student success, the education faculty, in turn, are challenged to model the facilitating role of the teacher. Achievement of our goals is realized when our facilitating faculty are able to provide the link among foundational content, pedagogical constructs, and authentic experiences.

In actualizing the conceptual framework through performance, we developed a Continuous Assessment Model that is a multifaceted system of accountability. Continuous assessment is a means of documenting the developmental growth patterns of the teacher education candidate throughout the schooling process (formative evaluation) and of ensuring the achievement of competencies identified for competent teaching (i.e., proficiency in teacher standards, successful completion of the National Teacher Examination or PRAXIS®, successful completion of the internship process, and the attainment of teacher certification), which is summative evaluation. Throughout the process of continuous assessment, multiple measures of performance assessment are designed for fair, flexible, and creative evaluation. As suggested by Kane and Khattri (1995), the key characteristics of performance assessment can be found in such modes as portfolios, on-demand performance tasks, projects, exhibitions, and teachers' structured observations. In the development of our Continuous Assessment Model, these performance measures were critical ingredients to the assessment process yielding valuable insights into assisting the development of the professional teacher.

For the institution, continuous assessment documents the effort by the teacher education program to produce a candidate who exhibits the competencies necessary for effective teaching based on the NTS. For the student, continuous assessment provides a record of competencies attained throughout the preparation process and produces a source of entries for an end product, the portfolio, which is evidence of the student's professional capabilities. In addition, the continuous assessment record provides baseline data for the development of a beginning teacher's professional development plan. For certification, continuous assessment provides additional documentation of the candidate's eligibility and not just a record of courses completed for the major.

The Continuous Assessment Model provides clearly defined, multiple performance measures and expected competencies to guide the preservice educator through the teacher preparation program at Asbury College. One of the performance-based measures embedded in the continuous assessment process is the preprofessional portfolio, used as part of a "gating procedure." The purpose of the gating procedure is to provide checkpoints of the candidate's progress, guided by the NTS as the students seek to attain the prescribed expectations for tomorrow's teacher.

Four gates provide checkpoints to monitor the progress of a teacher education candidate's mastery of the NTS. Each gate consists of criteria that the preservice educator must fulfill successfully to exit through the checkpoint. Gate criteria consist of formative and summative evaluation data which are reviewed at each of these checkpoints. These are:
- Gate 1 (Port of Entry)
- Gate 2 (Admission to Teacher Education)
- Gate 3 (Admission to Student Teaching)
- Gate 4 (Program Exit)

Program requirements, performance competencies, and portfolio components for each gate are identified. Program requirements consist mainly of summative evaluation data (e.g., entry/exit test scores; grade point averages; successful completion of courses in composition, mathematics, and oral communication; and faculty recommendations). As a means of validating the summative data, a performance measure of multiple tasks (i.e., student interview and portfolio review) is conducted at each gate.

At each gate, the portfolio assessment includes the ratings of the professional educator(s) and the self-ratings by the preservice educator. For both types of ratings, a common scoring rubric is used to evaluate the competence of the preservice professional against the New Teacher Standards (see examples in Tables 1 and 2). This scoring process provides a holistic evaluation of each standard and each candidate is measured against a 4-level rating scale of Accomplished, Proficient, Apprentice, and Novice. All candidates must attain a minimum of a Proficient ranking to meet each of the gate requirements.

If the committee decision is that a candidate does not meet the Proficient ranking in any of the assessment measures, the committee determines prescriptive strategies for remediation. The preservice student meets with the Department chair to create an action plan involving authentic experiences in response to the committee's recommendations. After completing the experiences designated by the action plan, the candidate must revisit the related checkpoint.

Using this model, we are assessing, concurrently, student competence, program and faculty accountability, and performance outcomes for institutional and accreditation purposes and using a mechanism for authentic validation for licensing. Within three years, we designed and implemented the model that resulted in a powerful assessment tool for programmatic coherence and ensuring the integrity of an authentic teacher preparation program. As a result of these efforts, Asbury's Education Department received the Innovative Teacher Preparation Award in 1995 from the Southeast Region of the Association of Teacher Educators.

Significance of Collaboration with P–12 Colleagues

At the heart of any awards or commendations is quality professional practice. Making a qualitative change in professional practice requires collegiality in modifying the scope and sequence of the training program and a willingness to tackle new approaches to instruction. As a faculty, we made a concerted effort to identify "best practice" for training teachers. For example, in our instructional program, one can observe the following new strategies: authentic assessment, cooperative learning, block scheduling of courses, extended field experiences, interdisciplinary instruction, integration of technology, and the development and use of portfolios. This is successfully accomplished by increased collaboration with P–12 educators and continually serves to strengthen our curriculum and our teaching practices.

The demands of implementing the Kentucky Education Reform Act were so intense that by its very nature, the cooperation of colleges and universities with P–12 schools was required. True systemic reform in P–12 schools cannot be realized without collaboration between public educators and the institutions preparing classroom teachers. A commitment to authenticity and professional performance requires ongoing interaction with teachers and students in P–12 schools.

In our restructured program, we intentionally included a new component, an exit performance event, to provide input to our program and our preservice candidates from our P–12 colleagues. This exit event occurs at the end of the student's professional semester and involves a 45-minute interview and portfolio review with a team of five educators consisting of one education faculty member, one discipline area faculty member, two public school teachers, and one public school administrator. Since its development three years ago, approximately 50 public school educators and administrators from five school districts have been trained and regularly participate in the exit interview.

As we were structuring this process, we did not envision all of the benefits that could result from this form of collaboration. Such benefits include the opportunity to experience a simulation of an employment interview, a review of the student's portfolio by public school educators, and the validation by professionals for licensure. Benefits to the training program include validation of our preparation process, feedback for program refinement, input for curricular revision, and the opportunity to develop collegial relationships with P–12 personnel. Last, the greatest delight has been the eager participation of our P–12 people and the level of ownership they have assumed for the success of our graduates and our program. Perhaps the greatest feature of the program is the true collaboration that occurs among administrators, classroom teachers, and college faculty.

Evaluation Embedded in Practice

Our primary objective is to provide a holistic training program that despite the traditional conventions of courses and credit hours creates a seamless web of preparation moving towards the stated goal, becoming a professional teacher. This holistic approach has been achieved by a high level of faculty collaboration to overcome duplication and unnecessary tasks with a focus on authenticity.

Within our performance assessment tasks, we attempt to focus on questions of importance that are faithful representations of various situations encountered in the real world of teaching as suggested by Wiggins (1993). Using the established criteria from the NTS, we expect preservice educators to use best teacher practice. Many of our course projects, on-demand performance tasks, and presentations include multiple approaches and address worthy problems of educational practice. Achieving authenticity for the preservice educator is a difficult task; however, we have attempted to address it in a variety of ways which extend across the preparation process.

Table 2. Portfolio Response to NTS via Continuous Assessment Model

Kentucky's New Teacher Standards	Gate 1 Evidence	Gate 2 Evidence	Gate 3 Evidence	Gate 4 Evidence
I (Designs/ Plans Instruction)	Initial Lesson Plan	Revised Lesson Plan	Lesson Plan Taught in Pre-Student Teaching Field Component	Lesson Plan Taught in Student Teaching
III (Implements and Manages Instruction)	Initial Field Component (observing instruction)	Advanced Field Component (assisting with instruction)	Methods Field Component (engaging in instruction)	Student Teaching Experience

Using the professional performance standards (NTS), a performance-based accountability system guides and reflects the progress of the teacher candidate. This is illustrated in Table 2 by providing examples of products and experiences a student prepares for the portfolio in response to the standards over time through the continuous assessment process. The students have the opportunity within the context of the standard to present item(s) that best illustrate their professional understanding while reflecting growth. Not only have the students received individual instructor feedback on each product, they also have had the opportunity for multiple responses from a broader professional context.

The NTS establish the framework for embedding performance criteria into our assessment practices in these areas:
- course development and explication,
- field-based experiences,

- Continuous Assessment Model,
- professional semester evaluation, and
- program evaluation.

Conclusion

As previously indicated, the NTS are an integral part of course delivery directly connected to the course objectives. Our students in their field-based experiences are evaluated by P–12 educators using an instrument which incorporates the NTS framework. An important component of the Continuous Assessment Model includes the portfolio that provides evidence of mastery of NTS competencies. Because we view the professional semester as the most authentic component of the preparation process, the student teaching evaluation instrument in its design totally embraces all of the NTS and the accompanying criteria. Since the entire training program revolves around the NTS, program evaluation is based on these premises and serves to guide the refinement process.

Few would conclude at Asbury College or in the surrounding school communities that the preparation of teachers is "business as usual." Students quickly perceive this is a demanding program requiring an intense level of commitment. Content faculty have been stimulated to evaluate their own practice and have sought assistance in preparing preservice teachers for teaching in schools undergoing reformation. Education faculty have been invigorated by redefining the training process to ensure authentic preparation. Public P–12 educators have become *bona fide* partners in meeting the challenge to engage preservice teachers in the reform efforts. The goals and expectations are high and can be achieved if we continue to press towards the mark of the high calling of preparing teachers to teach tomorrow's children.

References

Kane, M. B. & Khattri, N. (1995). Assessment reform: A work in progress. *Phi Delta Kappan, 77*(1), 30-36.
Wiggins, G. (1993). Assessment: Authenticity, context, and validity. *Phi Delta Kappan, 75*(3), 200-214.

ASHLAND UNIVERSITY

Mission: Possible

■

James Schnug and Ann Converse Shelly

We once heard a campus colleague declare that a university's mission statement should *not* be attainable. He considered such a statement as the ideal to which we strive but never reach, that our "reach should exceed our grasp" or programmatic complacency and short-sightedness may result. From our recent work in developing and operationalizing a mission statement for Ashland University's School of Education, this was an intriguing argument. But if an educational mission statement is a faraway, future focus (assuming we could even articulate such a future in this rapid-fire, changing field), then any faculty attempts at mission stating can, at best, be characterized as a never-ending game of "Mother, May I," and at its worst result in a wall-hanging that looks pretty next to the pictures but is only an *objet d'art* to which no one pays attention.

Through a series of collaborative ventures over the last five years, School of Education faculty at Ashland University have engaged in designing a mission statement that would corral and focus what we currently know is best for teacher education. Crucial to those attempts, however, was an honest, ongoing audit of talent, strengths, desires, and resources that tempered the realization of any stated "best practices." Mission stating continues to be a fluid process, wherein we can grasp what we reach for; in short, our own heavenly educational program. That fluid process also allows us to monitor and change our reach as new theory, practice, and resources emerge in the field of teacher education. For us, mission stating does not assume a product to strive for but a process to engage in, a process that allows foci to ebb and flow, shaping our work with university colleagues, school communities, and our teacher education students. In this chapter, we describe how this process of mission stating first began for us and how it continues today in our curriculum and program development.

Ashland University's School of Education

Ashland University is a private, Bretheran-affiliated liberal arts college in north central Ohio. Currently more than 1,800 undergraduate students are organized among four schools within 22 departments. Within the Ashland School of Education, the Teacher Education Department enrolls nearly 600 undergraduates who are working toward a Bachelor of Science degree in Education. Graduate education programs in curriculum and instruction, administration, supervision, and reading serve 2,000 students on the main campus and at three satellite university centers. A proposed Ed.D. program in Administration is currently awaiting approval from the Ohio Board of Regents. Last reaccredited at the basic and advanced level by National Council for the Accreditation of Teacher Education (NCATE) in 1992, the School of Education, staffed by 35 full-time professors, also continues to hold accreditation from Ohio.

The Process Begins

In 1990, the dean of the School of Education convened the teacher education department faculty to begin the NCATE reaccreditation process. A timeline was presented around the chronological themes of a "Year of Inquiry," a "Year of Implementation," and a "Year of Review." During the Year of Inquiry, the faculty organized across disciplines and specialties and began exploring and debating the main strands that should be infused across program coursework. Outside speakers, such as Linda Darling-Hammond and Thomas Lasley (University of Dayton), program students, and representatives from local school districts and the community also joined the discussions. During the year, 150 people engaged in more than 2,000 hours of study and discussion (Hughes & Whitted, 1991). Twenty-nine conceptual strands emerged and solidified into a working model of teacher education at Ashland University (see Table 1). Further delineation of the strands, as described by knowledge, skills, and attitude statements, eventually comprised the content of the program. Courses were audited, deleted, and developed according to the strands.

Table 1. Twenty-nine Strands From the Year of Inquiry

Teacher as Reflective Decision-Maker
Reflective Practitioner
Collaboration
Human Growth and Development
Learning Styles
Instructional Technology
Teaming Process
Creative Thinking
Instructional Methodology
Leadership Methodology
Classroom Management and Organization
Organizational Behavior
Theory and Research into Practice
Multicultural, Ethnic, Socioeconomic & Geographic Diversity, Gender
Interpersonal Communication Skills
Mastery of Oral and Written Language
Assessment and Evaluation of Student Learning
Instruction Based on Assessment, Intervention, Research, Learning Theory
Self-assessment and Self-evaluation
Assessment of School Programs
Content Mastery
Interdisciplinary Approach to Content
Valuing the Student
Learners with Exceptionalities
Students at Risk
Citizenship and Social Behavior
Changing Society and the Role of the Family
Issues, Trends, and Problems in Education
Professional Responsibilities
Legal, Ethical, and Moral Responsibilities

Distilling the Essence of a Program

A committee of faculty reviewed the strands and developed a draft mission statement. As in any synthesizing activity, much debate ensued as to what should be the essence of the teacher education program, even as that program was being elaborately described by the 29 strands. A model was finalized, "Teacher as Professional Educator." This model distilled three elements that characterized the program: current research informing teacher education, effective practice, and collaborative relationships among professors and public school faculty and staff. Further, eight tenets describing the skills of a professional educator were articulated and voted upon with the understanding that the 29 strands actualized those tenets. Table 2 displays the draft of the initial model.

Table 2. Draft Model – Teacher as Professional Educator – 1991

"Teacher as Professional Educator" & Supporting Tenets – 1991
The program is based on current research, effective practices, and dynamic, collaborative relationships among Ashland University faculty, Pre-K through grade 12 teachers, and administrators. The program is implemented through diverse experiences in university classes, field/clinical experiences, model sites, and professional development centers producing graduates who: 1. Can work in a cooperative, collaborative manner;   2. Are committed to lifelong learning;   3. Care about and value students;   4. Teach content and critical thinking skills through a student-centered approach;   5. Are reflective practitioners who begin with a knowledge of the teaching/learning process, curriculum content, child development, and children's social behavior in order to make effective and ethical decisions;   6. Believe all students can learn and succeed regardless of cultural background, gender, ability, and handicapping conditions;   7. Possess a knowledge base that links theory and research with practice; and   8. Are committed to scholarly responsibilities such as continued academic growth, professional memberships, and research, as well as to developing their certification fields.

The Focus Shifts to the Tenets

Following the Year of Inquiry, a Year of Implementation began during which faculty implemented the new and revised coursework of the new model, "Teacher as Professional Educator." Also during this time, NCATE visited the campus and accredited the unit under the new model. The 29 strands clearly articulated specific teacher education student attitudes, values, skills, and knowledge bases. Coursework evidenced these strands, yet faculty were concerned as to whether or not the model was making a difference programmatically, i.e., across courses. If the program said it would produce a "professional educator," how, as a faculty, would we know this was happening? This concern became the focus during the Year of Review.

Faculty once again organized, this time according to the eight tenets of the mission statement. Each group was charged with making any changes to their tenet and articulating levels of development that would serve as clear benchmarks, benchmarks that would evidence across courses that the tenet was being realized. Over four months, and seven drafts, the new mission statement emerged (see Table 3).

Table 3. Draft Model – Teacher as Professional Educator – 1995

"Teacher as Professional Educator" & Support Tenets – 1995
The AU Teacher Education program is based on current research, effective practice, and dynamic collaborative relationships among Ashland faculty, Pre-K through grade 12 teachers, and administrators. The program is implemented through diverse experiences in university classes, field/clinical experiences, model sites, and professional development centers. AU believes that a professional educator is a reflective practitioner who links practice with theory in the following ways: 1. Works cooperatively and collaboratively with all members of the educational community. 2. Communicates clearly and effectively through a variety of means. 3. Demonstrates understanding of human development, cultural diversity, socioeconomic influences, and learning differences, thereby enabling all children to learn and contribute. 4. Employs research in areas such as learning theory and instructional methodology. 5. Uses a variety of appropriate assessment techniques to enhance learning. 6. Masters appropriate disciplines so as to engage students in meaningful, active academic study. 7. Integrates educational technology in the teaching and learning process. 8. Assumes the lifelong responsibility to grow academically, professionally, and personally.

When compared to the original statement, it was evident that more emphasis was given to "technology" and "effective communication." Further, the concept of "reflective practitioner" (Schon, 1987) was moved to the opening paragraph, overtly highlighting this construct as a useful umbrella description of what a professional educator is. A quick perusal also revealed that "action verbs" became the stylistic choice of the faculty so that there could be a clearer delineation and description of the tenet beliefs. Benchmarks, such as those exemplified in Table 4, were also developed and revised for each of the tenet statements.

Although the Year of Review officially ended, new ventures approached and revealed the need to continue the mission stating process.

In particular, the state development of new licensure categories and an approaching NCATE review were catalysts for the use of the framework.

Table 4. Example of Tenet with Supporting Benchmark Levels – 1995

Tenet 5: Uses a variety of appropriate assessment techniques to enhance learning.

Level 1 Observes students and identifies assessment as a systematic collection of information about students.
Level 2 Identifies a variety of assessment techniques and how and why to use them.
Level 3 Achieves alignment (congruence) between instruction and assessment.
Level 4 Uses and interprets valid and reliable classroom assessments, both standardized and informal.
Level 5 Synthesizes assessment information to make instructionally beneficial decisions.
Level 6 Chooses, designs, and uses evaluation procedures for assessing programs and curricula.

A Living Document: A Year of Development

As we began the new academic year, the issue of how to use the tenets came to the fore. This was a critical part of keeping the tenets, benchmarks, and strands living and influential. The departmental curriculum committee developed guidelines for reviewing new courses and new programs that centered around the tenets. By making this process formal and mandatory, the tenets assumed major importance as Ashland University began to develop licensure programs to meet new state guidelines. (The state has assumed the role of consultant and partner, giving the institutions the power to develop programs *that emanate from the conceptual framework*.) While many institutions seem to have floundered at this point in the process, the tenets provided a base for us to ask what the ideal program in each area would look like. Each program used the tenets and benchmarks as well as the strands to guide development. Curriculum development started with a matrix based on the tenets.

The matrix allowed us to develop programs that reflected history and philosophy as well as best practice in a framework that we believe in strongly. Then, and only then, did we look beyond to the professional association guidelines and other external standards. These forces became a check, not a mandate. The tenets, among other forces, also became the base for the development of "common learnings" for the initial licensure programs. This is one example of the positive and constructive review and development process.

The conceptual framework also has provided a base for review and revamping of final assessment for all programs. This has had a significant impact on the assessment of student teaching and will have a backward impact on field experiences. If we want "X," we must grow toward it. This growth will include a role description for graduates based on the tenets and benchmarks as well as the strands. This philosophy will guide development of assessment portfolio guidelines. The impact of the Interstate New Teacher Assessment and Support Consortium (INTASC) and NCATE are being filtered through our own beliefs.

The importance of the tenets and the other elements of the conceptual framework mandates that they be open to review and revision at any time, not just on a timeline. The curriculum committee has developed guidelines for the initiation of a new tenet or a revision in a tenet. Any faculty member or group of faculty can propose changes following those guidelines. This year, these guidelines were tested with the proposal of a new tenet. The discussion has been open and frank with several alternatives proposed as a result of the debate. The result was an increased emphasis on the preamble to the tenets and new language that emphasizes the foundations of education. The use of the preamble in program review is now a part of the internal discussion.

Graduate programs have also been affected by the tenets, as they have been used to review the core of courses for all graduate programs. The graduate programs will play a significant role in the review of the benchmarks as we focus on the master teacher and on professional programs. The impact of the National Board for Professional Teaching Standards and the administration counterpart will be focused through the conceptual framework. The nature of the "living document" allows the impact of new elements in the field to be acknowledged and used.

Ashland University is committed to internal review as well as external accreditation. As the education programs approach the university's program review, we will be reviewing the tenets and related elements in light of the Ashland University mission, *Accent on the Individual*. Part of this review will focus on the "embeddedness" of teacher education in the institution. The use of the tenets as the basis of review will make that work more a self-check than simply a task to be done. All too often, such program evaluation is a matter of rote activity. At Ashland, we have set our sights on a specific target and can measure our effectiveness in terms of that goal.

The tenets have also served as a framework for our efforts to develop partnerships with the field. The Ashland City Schools/Ashland University Forum was developed as a way of identifying our mutual concerns. The tenets served as a basis for goal-setting and project evaluation for the forum. We are moving toward the development of a partnership with the Mansfield City Schools, and the framework, coherence, and focus of that effort will also grow from the tenets. In both cases, the projects selected have a direct relationship to the tenets that serve as the foundation of our work at the university.

Where Do We Go From Here?

Our commitment is to keeping the tenets and benchmarks as well as the strands alive. As we have grown, the implementation of program teams has made the use of the conceptual framework more critical than ever. The institution and its faculty value the discussion and debate that center around the tenets and even cherish the dissension that sometimes accompanies that debate. If we are truly committed to the beliefs expressed in the documents, we must continue to review and revise them as new information becomes available and as new faculty come to the community. We are dealing with the conundrum of an approved document with the stability that it gives to our programs versus the need to keep it alive and growing.

In the coming year, we will be reviewing the tenets, openly and formally. The benchmarks will be reviewed with the developmental nature of the profession as a base and the need to reach agreement on what the benchmarks mean to graduate and undergraduate programs alike. The need is to clarify the concepts, definitions, and the use of the benchmarks in program review. We also are looking at the reintegration of the strands in our model. The multidimensional nature of the three components is difficult to keep in mind as we implement the new programs, but it is essential. The increased importance of the preamble as a framework for programs and for a holistic review will be a challenge as well.

A Final Note

A living document sounds easy. The seven-year odyssey makes it clear that it is not. It is, in fact, uncomfortable and full of ambiguity. It has led to a beneficial sense of unease for faculty and administration. There is a certain cognitive dissonance for faculty as we use the framework. Ashland continually works to balance ongoing dialogue with implementation. The goal is to reach the point where this discussion and debate are as much a part of "faculty load" as teaching and scholarship. In short, only faculty work can render the "mission: possible."

References

Hughes, W. & Whitted, B. (1991, February). Year of inquiry at Ashland University. Paper presented at the Annual Meeting of the American Association of Colleges for Teacher Education, San Antonio, TX.

National Board for Professional Teaching Standards. (1991). *Toward high and rigorous standards for the teaching profession* (3rd ed.). Detroit, MI: Author.

National Council for Accreditation of Teacher Education. (1995). *Standards, procedures, and policies for the accreditation of professional education units*. Washington, DC: Author.

Ohio Department of Education. (1997). *Teacher education and licensure standards (Administrative Code Chapter 3301-24)*. Columbus, OH: Author.

Schon, D. (1987). *Educating the reflective practitioner*. San Francisco: Jossey-Bass.

CENTRAL MISSOURI STATE UNIVERSITY

One University's Journey
Toward Teacher Education Restructuring

■

Carol D. Mihalevich and Kathryn S. Carr

In this chapter, we chronicle the change process from a traditional teacher education program to an "assessment-as-learning" model at a medium-sized comprehensive state university having approximately 2,000 teacher education majors. We describe the process with six words that begin with the letter P. First is the Prologue or background information, then the Purposes or goals, followed by the Pain involved in the change process. Next we describe the Process itself, the Product or results to date, and finally the Prognosis as we reflect upon the outlook for the future.

Prologue

The 1990s were a decade of change in education at all levels. Central Missouri State University became a part of this movement that was widespread among institutions of learning, yet that each institution experienced in its own way. The seeds of change were in the wind long before the 1990s, however, through demands for accountability by industry, government, and the general public, as well as calls from private foundations for educational reform.

At Central, several major influences came together to shape the current change movement. One was the business model of Walter Deming; another was the growing acceptance of constructivist theories of education; the third was the related trend toward performance assessment, including the materials for educational change developed by Alverno College.

Rethinking the University's Role

From Deming's Total Quality Management (TQM) model comes the idea that the institution shares the responsibility for student learning. In application to education, it is the institution's responsibility to monitor student learning, provide frequent feedback, and structure learning experiences to meet the needs of the learners. These are not novel ideas in elementary education, but they are not common in colleges and universities. At Central, the philosophy spread from the College of Business and Economics by way of a FIPSE (Fund for Improvement of Postsecondary Education) grant in 1991 to a university-wide (although not universally accepted) project called Continuous Process Improvement (CPI).

Performance Assessment

According to the American Association for Higher Education (Astin *et al.*, 1992), hundreds of colleges and universities have established assessment programs at classroom, program, and institutional levels. Performance assessment encompasses a student's ability to integrate and apply learning across disciplines through some performance task. It involves higher-level cognitive functioning than traditional multiple-choice tests. Astin *et al.* continue:

> American colleges have a long history of grading and certifying student work. The more recent practice of assessment builds on that history by looking at student achievement not only within courses but across them, asking about cumulative learning outcomes. As a systematic process of gathering, interpreting, and using information about student learning, assessment is a powerful tool for educational improvement. (p. 1)

Support for performance assessment has come from a number of sources both inside and outside the institution. One internal influence has been the CPI project, whose motto is "Assessment as Learning" (Alverno College Faculty, 1994). CPI/FIPSE funds for faculty development have given approximately 60 of Central's faculty the opportunity to see performance assessment in action at Alverno College and provided for workshops conducted by Alverno faculty on Central's campus. Since 1991, Central faculty members from many disciplines who have visited Alverno College include at least five from the Department of Curriculum and Instruction. Through the adopt/adapt process, the CPI model departed in some ways from the one developed at Alverno; yet it seems fair to acknowledge that Alverno College was a major influence on Central's change process.

On April 21, 1993, the Faculty Senate passed a timetable for assessment implementation that said, in essence, that each department or faculty group responsible for a program will:

- identify and validate student learning outcomes for its programs by March 31, 1994;
- identify methods to assess student achievement and determine how the results of assessment will be used to improve student learning by November 30, 1994; and
- implement student assessment, documenting how the results are used to improve student learning by November 30, 1995.

Another factor that relates directly to Central's teacher education program is the influence of the state's Department of Elementary and Secondary Education as well as P–12 schools. The Missouri Outstanding Schools Act of 1993 is a state initiative that is driving revision of statewide assessment toward a system of performance assessment. State certification requirements for teachers are also moving in this direction.

Another argument for performance assessment at all levels is that the mode of assessment selected should be consistent with the instructional model followed. As Marzano *et al.* (1993) note, there is a growing emphasis on active learning, problem-solving, and the integration of curricula in today's classrooms. They reason that consistency with an active-learning instructional model requires similar types of assessment tasks.

Active Learning

Constructivism has had a major impact on early childhood, elementary, and secondary education and is the prevailing theory embraced by many teacher educators, including ours. Constructivism, to put it simply, is a theory of active learning stemming from cognitive psychology, including the work of Piaget, Vygotsky, and American pioneers in education such as Dewey. As Duckworth (1987) summarizes the theory, teachers may teach, but unless the student organizes the information in his/her own way, associates it with some prior experience, and makes it his or her own, learning has not occurred. Readers of Vygotsky also add the idea that knowledge is socially constructed, and therefore, students need opportunities to discuss their learning with others through various cooperative structures.

Table 1 (adapted from Barnes, 1992) shows the types of changes in instruction and the role of instructors to which the teacher education program at Central aspires.

Table 1. Changes in Teaching and Learning

Change From:	Change To:
Transmission Model	Transaction Model
Teacher Dispenses Knowledge	Learner Constructs Knowledge
Passive Listening	Active Learning
Teacher-Centered	Student-Centered
Teacher Responsibility	Student Responsibility
Acquisition of Knowledge	Application, Analysis, and Critical Thinking
Assessment of Fact Recall	Performance Assessment and Problem-Solving
Competition Among Students	Peer and Teacher Collaboration
Course-Credit Model	Competency-Based Validation

To summarize, the influences of TQM/CPI and Alverno College, performance assessment, and belief in the constructivist theory of active learning all contributed to the commitment to change teacher education at Central.

Purposes

In January 1993, faculty in the Department of Curriculum and Instruction elected to join the university's Continuous Process Improvement (CPI) project and set out to restructure teacher education at Central. We began developing a "systems" approach to education where a seamless P–16 educational program would be available to every student. With this vision came the realization that faculty in teacher education are responsible for the development of a new breed of educator—one who can foster active learning, multiple intelligences, critical thinking, and global perspectives; can align curriculum and assessment; and can apply this knowledge in the restructuring of schools. The immediate purposes of the restructuring plan are summarized as:

1. To identify program and specific outcomes for the teacher education program; the general student learning outcomes focused on Knowledge, Skills, and Attitudes (KSAs) in the areas of Communicating, Valuing, Thinking, and Social Interaction, which were consistent with CPI university-wide outcomes; and the outcomes for the teacher education major of School and Instructional Organization and Global Awareness;
2. To align program outcomes with those of the university, state accrediting agency, national accrediting bodies, and professional organizations;
3. To structure the sequences of learning experiences in such a way as to enable students to become competent in the program outcomes;
4. To devise benchmarks and assessment for monitoring student progress; and
5. To change teaching and assessment toward an active-learning model.

Pain

Institutional change inevitably involves some degree of discomfort for the participants, if not sheer pain. Some of the growing pains we experienced were of this nature, while others might have been avoided. We will describe a few of the trials experienced by the department, with a focus on a group of ten early childhood, elementary, and middle school education methods instructors who met an average of three times a month for four years.

Problems fell into the following categories: the Nay-Sayers, Natural Discomfort, Time Factors and Distractions, and the Difficulty of the Task.

The Nay-Sayers. Central's teacher education program has enjoyed a reputation for quality since the founding of the institution as a Normal Training School in 1875. In the 1970s and 1980s, the program was especially successful, and so some faculty members saw no reason to change. The objections of the Nay-Sayers were typical of resistance to change: "It won't work here," "Our institution is too large," "We tried that years ago," and "I've seen many fads come and go."

Natural Discomfort. Then there were the realities of the change process. Each of us probably felt somewhat threatened when our beliefs were challenged, and we gave up the security of some long-held practices to try something new. Another natural cause of tension was an initial attempt at collaboration for people accustomed to working autonomously. In other words, we had too many cooks who each thought they had the best recipe for curriculum design.

Time Factors and Distractions. Time limitations and distractions were major sources of frustration. Although we seemed to accomplish the most during off-campus retreats, we settled on meetings held from 11 a.m. – 1 p.m. several times a month. To facilitate planning, the department chair scheduled no classes during this two-hour period.

Often there were other matters to discuss—e.g., preparing for NCATE or state accreditation visits—and we left the meeting feeling frustrated over the lack of accomplishment. Sometimes other professional obligations such as the preparation of annual reports and promotion dossiers, publication deadlines, or meetings of other committees led to failure to prepare adequately for meetings.

Difficulty of the Task. The task itself was daunting. It was hard to know where to begin. Also, it was difficult to visualize the end product because there were few models to follow of state universities with programs as large as ours.

Process

Development of Outcomes

The first step in the process was to ensure that the faculty had the same vision. What would a comprehensive assessment-as-learning program look like? We began in September 1993 with a three-day retreat with Kathryn Henn-Reinke, a faculty member from Alverno College, as facilitator for our committee of ten faculty, three public school administrators, and three public school practitioners. We left the retreat energized, with a grasp of the conceptual shift necessary to design a program focusing on outcomes, and with our first rough draft of program outcomes in hand.

During the next academic year, we spent many long hours of philosophical discussion of the knowledge, skills, and attitudes (KSAs) that represent the ideal teacher. The committee met regularly during the 1993–94 academic year to revise our draft of program outcomes, to align them with the four university studies outcomes, and to delineate an extensive list of KSAs across education courses.

Outcomes Validation

We sent a survey with copies of our draft program and course outcomes to colleagues at professional organizations and sister institutions, public school administrators and practitioners, and preservice teachers. The survey requested respondents to rate each outcome denoting the importance of the competency on a five-point Likert scale. They also were asked to suggest additional competencies which they felt were important. The data were analyzed, and as a result, some outcomes were deleted, revised for clarity, or added as recommended.

Curricular Evaluation

The next year was spent evaluating our courses to determine where the KSAs were being taught in our program and the level of competency attained in each course. We developed a curriculum matrix to ensure that every outcome was taught in appropriate increments across the courses. We found that some were totally overlooked while others were taught at the same level of competency in several courses. In addition, we examined the four university outcomes to identify entry-level skills for the teacher education program and ways these skills would be enhanced throughout our program.

Assessment System

The committee's most recent task was to develop a system for comprehensive assessment where both faculty and students could determine student proficiency in outcomes at program entry; developmental benchmarks would provide evidence of student growth in knowledge, skills, and attitudes throughout the professional program; and an exit-level assessment would complete the system.

Product

"Product" really should be plural because there have been a number of positive results of our four-year study. First is our progress toward restructuring the teacher education program. Outcomes have been identified, validated, sequenced, and aligned with university-wide outcomes. We have begun to identify benchmarks and assessments for entry and exit level, and for monitoring students progress through the program. These evaluations will provide the documentation for both student goal-setting and validation of proficiency in program outcomes.

As part of structuring learning experiences, our goal is to provide preservice teachers with a graduated entry into the profession. We revised the field experiences to focus on program competencies, developed rubrics with explicit criteria, and required reflective assessment of professional knowledge at varying levels of competency in classrooms, day care and nursery settings, and after-school programs. Finally, we sequenced the clinical experiences to ensure progression of competency attainment so that students move from observation exercises to whole-class instruction. Also, through a state grant, we have developed a professional development school partnership with two area P–12 schools that will multiply our students' opportunities for field experiences. Through workshops where teachers and university faculty develop a common knowledge base, we will be able to coordinate field experiences and our coursework on campus.

A distinct change has occurred in the philosophy and teaching of the faculty. We now exhibit most of the changes that Barnes (1992) recommended. Our teaching is more student-centered. There is more inquiry and less lecture, more reflective thinking, application, and integration of learning throughout. Performance assessment in coursework now supplements or replaces multiple-choice tests.

As we focused on competency attainment and clustering of outcomes across the program, course boundaries began to disappear. We offered our first integrated block of methods courses in the spring 1997 semester. Next year, we plan to offer two integrated methods blocks, one for early childhood/lower elementary and another for upper elementary/middle school.

Prognosis

The prognosis appears very positive. Yes, there is still much work to do, but we have pulled the wagon over the hill, and now the journey looks much easier. Plans for summative evaluation call for an electronic portfolio in which students will document their attainment of benchmarks through videos of their teaching, lesson plans, and other products. We have yet to communicate program outcomes, which is more than just an essential aspect of public relations. Student awareness of outcomes and advance knowledge of rubrics is the cornerstone of the assessment-as-learning model.

Lessons Learned

We conclude with a summary of the lessons learned on our journey toward restructuring teacher education. One caution we offer is to limit the scope of the project. It seems now that we tackled too much at once and identified too many specific outcomes. Designing professional development for ourselves and negotiating a shared vision among the faculty were necessary before beginning to identify outcomes. Time for planning is essential; however, the project should not drag on so long that the faculty becomes discouraged. The validation of outcomes by asking others to review them and conducting a program evaluation to determine what is actually taught are also important steps. The next step is developing a comprehensive system of benchmarks and performance assessments. Finally, we recommend a plan for communicating the program to others. But there is no "last" step, because the journey to improve teacher education never ends.

References

Alverno College Faculty. (1994). *Student assessment-as-learning at Alverno College*. Milwaukee, WI: Alverno Productions.

Astin, A., Banta, T., Cross, P., El-Khawas, E., Ewell, P., Hutchings, P., Marchese T., McClenney, K., Mentkowski, M., Miller, M., Moran, T., & Wright, B. (1992). *Principles of good practice for assessing student learning*. Washington, DC: American Association for Higher Education.

Barnes, D. (1992). *From communication to curriculum*. Portsmouth, NH: Heinemann.

Duckworth, E. (1987). *The having of wonderful ideas and other essays on teaching and learning*. New York: Teachers College Press.

Marzano, R., Pickering, D., and McTighe, J. (1993). *Assessing student outcomes*. Alexandria, VA: Association for Supervision and Curriculum Development.

Assessment: A Process

■

Virginia C. Nelms and Marilyn G. Thomas

Clayton College & State University (CCSU) is a senior-level institution in the University System of Georgia. The Middle-Level Teacher Education Program was begun in summer 1992 with teams of public school administrators, classroom teachers, arts and sciences faculty, and outside consultants developing a program framework solely for the preparation of middle-level teachers. A Philip Morris *Teaching for Tomorrow* grant in association with Alverno College permitted us to work with other colleges defining program outcomes and assessments. Several characteristics distinguish this outcome-focused program from other teacher preparation programs:

- the program is in the School of Arts and Sciences, allowing concepts and pedagogical preparation for teacher candidates to be integrated;
- the program is highly field-based, thus requiring a close collaboration between public school educators and university faculty in concepts and pedagogy preparation; and
- the program provides a year-long internship in an assigned school site where teacher candidates experience an academic school year under the guidance and support of a mentor teacher and other school faculty.

Program governance is by committees of arts and sciences faculty and mentor teacher clinical faculty.

During program development, we asked an overarching question: "What should a middle-level teacher know and be able to do?" Middle school educators and arts and sciences faculty spent many hours collaborating on what a teacher needs to know and what experiences should support that content knowledge. Likewise, collaboration between college and school faculties led to the field experiences which support and expand this knowledge. Preservice teachers are placed in P–12 classrooms early and often in continued cooperation with the college's partner schools. Student and program assessments are an integral part of program design. The ongoing nature of collaboration defines our program culture as one which requires faculty continually to evaluate and modify coursework and field experiences to address the students' needs.

From a review of standards for various national organizations and the ten essential elements of a "true" middle school as endorsed by the National Middle School Association (*This We Believe*, 1992), the following guiding principles were established:

- All components of the program will be established in outcome-focused, assessment-based terminology and will be designed to enhance student learning.
- All outcomes will be assessed by performance in a variety of settings and modes.

Continued study and discussion resulted in six outcomes. These outcomes form the philosophical foundation of the program (see Table 1) and have been incorporated into course and program design, teaching, and assessments. Throughout the program, students are encouraged to ask themselves about their progress in relation to the program outcomes. This introspection forms the basis for self-assessment and reflection.

Students are admitted to the program as a cohort group, and throughout the six quarters of the program, they participate in collaborative learning activities which simulate the interdisciplinary team approach of middle schools. Upon entrance to the program, students indicate their preferences for primary and secondary areas of academic concentrations. Four academic areas are available for concentration: language arts, mathematics, science, and social studies. During the fall quarter of the junior year, students work in an interdisciplinary team on group activities and design of a teaching unit. Since most middle school teachers may have to teach in any one of the four academic areas, all students are required to take an upper-division course in each academic area. In addition to these courses, students must take two additional courses in their secondary area of concentration and five additional courses in their primary area.

Table 1. Teacher Education Program Outcomes

The Teacher Education Program Outcomes come from the knowledge base that has been approved for the Middle-Level Education degree. The outcomes are written to address what graduates should know and be able to do upon completion of the program.

1. **Diagnoses Learning Needs**. The graduate uses a variety of assessment techniques and utilizes appropriate technologies to gather information about students and integrates this information to determine learners' strengths and areas to be developed.

2. **Plans for Student Learning**. The graduate integrates knowledge of discipline content, the nature of the learners, learning theories, instructional strategies, and state/local curriculum guides to plan instruction.

3. **Facilitates Student Learning**. The graduate implements plans with flexibility and is guided by knowledge of discipline content, the nature of the learners, learning theories, and instructional strategies.

4. **Demonstrates Appropriate Knowledge**. The graduate has general knowledge across a broad spectrum of liberal arts and sciences and possesses discipline-specific knowledge at a level appropriate for the chosen teaching field.

5. **Fosters Student Well-Being to Support Learning**. The graduate interacts with students, school colleagues, parents, and agencies in the larger community to foster student well-being and learning.

6. **Assumes the Role of Professional Educator**. The graduate acts in accordance with the structure, standards, and responsibilities of the profession and recognizes the role of the school in supporting a democratic society.

The program is designed so that during the six quarters of the junior and senior years, students have opportunities to observe and teach in middle school settings. Courses are taught cooperatively by arts and sciences faculty and practicing classroom teachers. Arts and sciences content courses in the junior year have a pedagogy lab, and registration in the courses stipulates, in addition to the class time devoted to learning the discipline, students will participate in the pedagogy labs. Public school educators and arts and sciences faculty work together in preparing labs which focus on theory and practice, including how discipline content is taught in middle schools.

Throughout five of the six quarters of the program, students take a seminar, a one-hour institutional credit course, in education. During each quarter of the junior year, this seminar meets once a week and serves as an introduction to the partnership schools and the concept of interdisciplinary teaming. Through this seminar, students also begin to identify their individual strengths and learning styles. Emphasis is placed upon translating this knowledge to the classroom—to teaching, learning, and self-assessment. An integral part of the course is a journal or log containing reflections on observations and activities. Additionally, students are introduced to the concept of the program portfolio as a systematic way to collect evidence for reflection and analysis of professional growth and progression toward program outcomes. At CCSU, portfolios have been defined as selective collections of evidence that program outcomes have been achieved.

In fall of the junior year, students begin to collect evidence supporting the work they do with adolescents and begin to assess the reasons why they want to work with middle-level learners. This forms the beginnings of a philosophy paper presented to the faculty during the senior-year exit interview and program portfolio presentation. In discussions with students, emphasis is placed on continually refining portfolio evidence to show achievement of program outcomes. Through discussions and conferences, students make continual selections of this evidence for the program portfolio—a significant assessment component of the program.

In program and course development, assessment as an integral part of each course as well as the program was paid careful attention. During content course work, students maintain portfolios which include evidence of course experiences, written assignments, unit and lesson plans, video- and audio-taped teaching episodes, reflections on observations and teaching episodes (journals), and evidence of professional readings.

During winter and spring quarters of the junior year, principals and teachers in the partner schools instruct the CCSU students in the nature of the learner and instructional strategies appropriate for middle-level learners. These courses, designed by practicing administrators and teachers, are taught on-site in middle schools. Throughout the junior year, students work in cooperative groups, participate in extensive middle school observations and experiences, and interact with middle-level teachers and students. Additionally, they observe faculty modeling team teaching, develop interdisciplinary units, and begin to utilize technology as a part of coursework. Students are asked to reflect on how assessment relates to teaching and learning, and an emphasis is placed upon viewing assessment as learning.

Beginning with a student's admission to the program, checkpoints determine his or her advancement. Program admission requires an academic and program grade point average of 2.5 on a scale of 4.0, a minimum grade of C in each course, a writing assessment, documented work with children, minimum competence with computers, and attendance at a group orientation session. Once a student is admitted to the program, the Professional Education Program Committee (PEPC) reviews and monitors his or her progress. During the junior year, students must successfully complete all coursework with a grade of C or better, begin a program portfolio, achieve the teacher education writing profile, demonstrate competence in oral communication, and receive the recommendation/endorsement of the arts and sciences and school-based faculties.

In an off-site work session, faculty developed the criteria for evaluating academic and fieldwork during the student's junior year. While grades in individual courses are one piece of evidence of content knowledge, they seldom indicate the student's ability to work collaboratively and put that knowledge to use. Since individual courses are developed with a focus on the program outcomes of fostering knowledge of the discipline and collaboration, coupled with the development of a professional demeanor, it became apparent to faculty that an assessment indicating these areas of growth was needed. Evidence of each student's progress is indicated at the end of each quarter of the junior year. Professional growth proceeds along a continuum, with faculty assessment, student reflection, and self-assessment as integral components. Viewing assessment as learning encourages students and faculty to work cooperatively in determining where the student is on the continuum of becoming a professional. Faculty and students continue to work on making criteria explicit.

During program development, faculty decided that performance assessment should be an integral part of classes. Performance assessment and performance-based instruction are complementary processes (the Durden and Hunt chapter gives further illustration of this). The first step in designing performance-based instruction is to decide what we want students to be able to do with what they learn. Explicit criteria for student performance, and the inclusion of performance-based assessment, have helped move the program from a product- to a process-based orientation and have helped emphasize assessment as learning.

As students approach the end of the junior year (their first year in the program), they participate in a "Portfolio Fair." They exhibit evidence collected during the year which meets program outcomes. This informal activity is designed to keep the collection of evidence toward program outcomes as the central focus of the student's progress. The program portfolio should represent the student's growth in achieving program outcomes and become a way of communicating for students and faculty. As students proceed with portfolio preparation, they continually ask themselves, "How has what I am learning helped me achieve the program outcomes?" Working with and observing students in portfolio preparation helps the faculty understand individual growth and learning.

Mentor teachers working with the coordinator of field experiences and faculty in the content areas have developed the experiences and assessments for the senior internship. The internship provides students the opportunity to develop professional attitudes and dispositions as they learn how to apply knowledge and make professional decisions, and it presents a setting for demonstrating evidence of professional knowledge, attitudes, and skills.

During the year-long internship, there are two opportunities at mid-quarter and at end-of-quarter for formal assessments through conferences. These conferences focus on the knowledge and skills demonstrated by the interns with an emphasis on reflection and self-assessment. Conferences provide an opportunity for the intern, mentor, and college coordinator to discuss progress and set goals for the next period of work. Assessment focuses primarily on the intern's readiness for full-time involvement in the assigned school site.

Since our program follows a developmental model, the full-time spring quarter internship provides opportunities for interns to assume progressive degrees of responsibility. The mentor teachers and field coordinator synthesize feedback from a variety of external sources and combine this with the interns' continual self-assessment of goals and progress toward the program outcomes. Assessment focuses on evidence of the interns' knowledge and skills in recognizing the diversity of learners in their classrooms and demonstrating the ability to address the needs of these learners.

During spring quarter, interns provide individual portfolios of professional knowledge and skills for assessing readiness to exit the program. The portfolio includes selected evidence of the intern's readiness to make sound professional decisions regarding students' welfare and to provide effective learning experiences on the basis of that diagnosis. It also includes evidence of the intern's ability to interact and collaborate with parents, colleagues, and administrators and to meet student needs. The portfolio provides lesson plans, video- and audio-taped instruction, self-assessments and reflections, mentor feedback, and student work samples as evidence of effective instruction focusing on successful student performance. The portfolio includes evidence of monitoring and analyzing student performance as well as of the intern's own growth. The exit interview, where the portfolio is presented, is an opportunity for interns to demonstrate professional knowledge and skills to an audience of educators who were involved in their professional development. This is a collaborative effort by multiple parties: the mentor teacher, building principal, arts and sciences faculty, and program coordinator.

During the first two years of program development, mentor teachers, arts and sciences faculty, and program coordinators worked together to determine the experiences and assessments that would provide the most useful feedback for students regarding their professional growth and development in the competencies of the teaching profession. The program outcomes describe the knowledge and skills demonstrated by a successful graduate of the program. The assessment experiences are opportunities for students and experienced educators to share regular feedback on the professional progress of the interns. The final assessment of professional knowledge and skills is the responsibility of the program coordinator and the program steering committee (PEPC). This allows for comprehensive assessment and documentation of the individual intern's knowledge and skills according to the program outcomes.

In keeping with the concept that assessment is an ongoing process, a plan to evaluate the program has been developed. An external advisory committee composed of teachers, school system administrators, graduates, and faculty will meet biannually. The committee reviews course sequencing and activities, school-based field experiences, internship activities, and program assessment. This plan assures program continuity and helps keep assessment at the core of student and program development.

The process of continuing to develop outcomes and assessments is demanding and time-consuming, but we all agree that it is a worthwhile endeavor. Faculty members from arts and sciences and partner schools continue to meet to discuss, plan, and write assessments, and, in this process, we learn and share. We believe the process is worth the time and effort required.

References

Carnegie Council on Adolescent Development. (1990). *Turning points: Preparing American youth for the 21st century: Recommendation for transforming middle grade schools*. Washington, DC: Author.

National Middle School Association. (1992). *This we believe*. Columbus, OH: Author.

CLAYTON COLLEGE & STATE UNIVERSITY - II

Outcomes and Assessment
in Language Arts and Mathematics

■

Debra Durden and Annita Hunt

The Middle-Level Teacher Education Program at Clayton College & State University (CCSU) is an outcome-focused, assessment-based, learner-centered partnership with the School of Arts and Sciences and the school systems in CCSU's service area. Teacher Education Program Outcomes form the foundation for what students will be able to do upon completion of the program (see table of outcomes and chapter by Nelms and Thomas). Course outcomes mesh with program outcomes, and together they provide the basis for teaching and assessment.

Faculty teaching in the program have determined that traditional tests, while having a place in assessment, are not the only way to assess student learning. To teach and thus assess in middle school, students must have experienced authentic assessment. Assessment should not only demonstrate what a learner knows but show how the learner can perform, apply, and integrate knowledge.

One way to demonstrate what a learner knows is to use performance assessment, which consists of evaluations of a student's behavior while performing a task which is authentic, or as close as possible to what we want students to be able to do. Performance criteria are stipulated and rubrics for acceptable and unacceptable performance are established. Based upon these tenets, CCSU's middle-level program incorporates authentic assessments which are aligned with program outcomes, course outcomes, and student involvement. This chapter describes course outcome development and assessment in two discipline areas of CCSU's Middle-Level Teacher Education Program.

Outcomes and Assessment in Mathematics

The process of developing course outcomes and appropriate ways to assess those outcomes is not a linear process. One knows what a course should be and what it should accomplish and that the *course* outcomes should contribute to the achievement of the *program's* outcomes. One also knows that the assessments should be an integral part of the course, reflect the manner in which the concepts are taught, and be learning experiences. Determining how to accomplish these goals involves trial and error, reflection, and reevaluation.

In 1993, the development of a "Concepts of Geometry" course for program juniors was not terribly difficult. The National Council of Teachers of Mathematics (NCTM) had recently published a set of K–12 standards, and materials were being produced to help implement those standards. Thus, given CCSU's commitment to outcomes assessment and the receptivity of its Mathematics Department to the incorporation of NCTM's recommendations, the standards were easily adapted to college-level instruction at CCSU. What seemed difficult was the task of writing course outcomes. Our Alverno *Teaching for Tomorrow* team simplified the task tremendously by explaining that the course outcomes were just that— *course* outcomes. Since the course had been developed to fit the Teacher Education Program Outcomes, its outcomes would naturally contribute to the achievement of the program's outcomes. But the course outcomes themselves did not have to be a subset of the program outcomes. With that clarification, it was easy to formulate the list of outcomes for the "Concepts of Geometry" course.

The primary purpose of the course should be to provide students with a strong base of content knowledge (Program Outcome IV: Demonstrates Appropriate Knowledge). Therefore, the first course outcome became: *The student who successfully completes this course has a workable foundation in the concepts of geometry appropriate for middle grades instruction.* Because the junior-level courses in CCSU's teacher education program are supposed to combine subject-matter content with pedagogy, a secondary purpose of the course was to teach students how to teach geometry. Educational research indicates that teachers teach as they were taught and that students learn mathematics best by being actively involved in doing mathematics. Therefore, the second outcome became: *The student who successfully completes this course will have encountered new learning experiences through exploration and discovery and opportunities for broadening perspectives.* Students in the course would work actively and collaboratively, using technology and other means to explore concepts, stretching their minds, and learning to reflect and communicate with others. By incorporating these methods in their own teaching, graduates of the program will be able to facilitate student learning (Program Outcome III).

By studying the widely-accepted van Hiele theory of how students learn geometry and incorporating that theory into the creation of a geometry lesson for middle school students, the program graduate will be able better to diagnose learning needs (Program Outcome I) and plan for student learning (Program Outcome II). Thus, the third outcome for the "Concepts of Geometry" course became: *The student who successfully completes the course can identify levels of geometric understanding described by the van Hiele model and design lessons accordingly.*

The fourth and final outcome for the "Concepts of Geometry" course is: *The student who successfully completes the course is able to reflect on the pedagogy used in class and in labs based on NCTM's standards for middle grades teaching.* A vital component of CCSU's teacher education program is its partnership with area school systems. An essential feature of the junior-level mathematics courses in the program is the use of practicing middle school teachers as adjunct faculty who conduct six to eight pedagogy labs per quarter for each of these courses. Students in the geometry course study the recommendations that were demonstrated in that lab. At the end of the quarter, they are asked to turn in those reflections along with a critique of the course with respect to its outcomes and/or its implementation of the NCTM standards. It is not enough to model appropriate teaching strategies; students must be led to an awareness of those strategies to enhance the chances of their implementing them in their own teaching, thus facilitating student learning (Program Outcome III).

The development of instruments and techniques for the assessment of the course outcomes is an evolutionary process and differs slightly each quarter. Because the majority of learning in this course takes place on the computer (with Geometer's Sketchpad® software), assessments should reflect that fact. Therefore, the midterm and final assessments are composed primarily of computer explorations that extend and require synthesis of classroom experiences. For example, students might be given a problem such as:

The figure below was constructed using the given script. Use Sketchpad® to reproduce the figure.

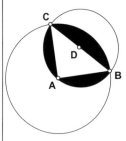

Given:
1. Point A
2. Point B

Steps:
1. Let [j] = Segment between Point B and Point A.
2. Let [1] = Circle with center at Point A passing through Point B.
3. Let [j'] = Image of Segment [j] rotated 90.000 degrees about center Point A.
4. Let [C] = Intersection of Circle [1] and Segment [j'].
5. Let [k] = Segment between Point B and Point [C].
6. Let [D] = Midpoint of Segment [k].
7. Let [2] = Circle with center at Midpoint [D] passing through Point B.

Then:
a.   Calculate the area of the shaded regions and explain your procedure. [*Note*: Your procedure is what I am most interested in, so please give a detailed explanation.] Save your work to your disk.
b.   What is the relationship among the areas of the shaded regions? Why?

Students in this course also create a middle school mathematics lesson that incorporates Sketchpad® as well as instructional strategies recommended by NCTM and the van Hiele theory of how students learn geometry. Students help generate the criteria by which these projects are assessed, but those criteria vary slightly from class to class. The list might include the following:
• Promotes exploration
• Is mathematically sound
• Uses Sketchpad® effectively
• Has educational value
• Serves differing ability levels
• Promotes critical thinking
• Promotes creativity
• Incorporates the van Hiele theory

Before presenting their projects, students work in pairs to assess each other's projects. Presentations are videotaped and self-assessed. Those videotapes and an abstract describing the lesson are candidates for inclusion in each student's program portfolio. Students also present problem solutions to the class. A number of those presentations are videotaped and are assessed by the instructor and self-assessed by the students.

Other experiences aid the students to broaden their perspectives on mathematics. Students in the course are required to read *Flatland*, a social satire about life in a two-dimensional world, written in 1884 by Edwin A. Abbott. After reading and discussing the book, they are asked to write an essay or to respond to a series of short discussion topics that relate their reading to teaching and to the Teacher Education Program Outcomes. For example, students might be asked to respond to the following:

> Relate the statement "to be self-contented is to be vile and ignorant, and ... to aspire is better than to be blindly and impotently happy" (p. 75) to CCSU's Teacher Education Program Outcomes and to you as a teacher.

Other assessment practices are implemented in the "Number Concepts" and "Concepts of Algebra" courses, the other junior-level mathematics courses for teacher education majors. Students study NCTM recommendations for the teaching of number concepts and of algebra and prepare mini-lessons that incorporate recommended strategies. In addition to paper-and-pencil tests, performance tests in the use of appropriate manipulatives are given in these courses. Pedagogy labs, as well as classroom experiences, are reflected upon in logs that are turned in for a grade. In all courses, communication skills, reflection, and conceptual understanding are emphasized and assessed. Assessment is an integral part of each course, and its purpose is to provide an opportunity for students to demonstrate their level of understanding and to synthesize what they have learned, thus creating a new level of understanding.

Outcomes and Assessment in Language Arts

In developing courses for the language arts major in teacher education, arts and sciences faculty and classroom teachers from CCSU's partner schools agreed that a strong content or knowledge component, as well as a strong pedagogy component that allows for interaction with real teachers in and from middle-level classrooms, would provide both the knowledge and process necessary to effectively prepare future middle-level language arts teachers. Faculty also recognized the need for modeling strategies that would address the diverse individual learning styles of teacher education students, and, in turn, the various learning styles of their future students. Delivery of language arts content using diverse strategies and integration of the necessary language arts skills through a literature-based program seemed to best reflect the process approach necessary to help students successfully achieve both course and program outcomes.

Using the National Council of Teachers of English (NCTE) and International Reading Association (IRA) standards, the Georgia Quality Core Curriculum (QCC) objectives, and the CCSU General Education (university-wide) outcomes of Communication and Critical Thinking as a foundation, the curriculum committee adapted language arts content for reading, writing, listening, speaking, and comprehension of literary elements for each course envisioned, working to provide the depth and breadth of knowledge and skill necessary for a well-rounded language arts teacher of middle grades. Following that task, the committee then turned to the development of course objectives and assessments by which students would demonstrate the achievement of knowledge and skills in these areas, knowing that assessments must be learning experiences in themselves.

For example, in developing the "Reading and Writing Workshop" course, faculty realized that students need a strong knowledge of the reading and writing processes, but they also need to learn how to teach reading and writing skills to middle-level learners. Therefore, the first course outcome is: *The teacher education student will demonstrate mastery of the writing process as evidenced in his/her own writing,* and a subsequent outcome states: *The teacher education student will create activities to teach the writing process and will implement these activities in a middle school language arts classroom.* These two course outcomes are tied directly to Program Outcome II: Plans for Student Learning, Program Outcome III: Facilitates Student Learning, and Program Outcome IV: Demonstrates Appropriate Knowledge. Students improve their own writing skills while studying the writing process and how to use it effectively with their middle level students. They peer-edit just as their students will in the future, and they assess their own writings and the writings of others using the CCSU writing criteria. In other words, they learn assessment and self-assessment techniques for each strategy by employing these assessment techniques in their own writing practice. Thus, assessing writing is an integral part of the course, with students experiencing assessment both as student and as future teacher.

Because reading skills and strategies are also included in the knowledge base for this course, course outcome #3 for the "Reading and Writing Workshop" states: *The teacher education student will demonstrate knowledge of effective reading strategies that will improve the reading comprehension and vocabulary skills of middle-level learners.* Once again, this course outcome is tied to Program Outcomes II, III, and IV. Language arts teacher education students learn how to apply strategies effectively by actually using them to read and to study the content for the reading and writing workshop course. In addition, students are placed in cooperative groups and carry out many assignments within those groups, just as middle-level students might be required to do when reading both literature and text content material.

Just as the course outcomes above focus on the facilitation of student learning (i.e., Program Outcome III), so do the other outcomes for the course, which deal with the skills and strategies used when teaching and learning literary elements, critical thinking skills, oral language skills, and grammar skills. (For example, *the teacher education student will demonstrate the ability to integrate the teaching of various communication and critical thinking skills by using literature of interest to the middle-level learner*). Therefore, in all junior-level courses, not only is pedagogy emphasized in the regular class blocks, but pedagogy labs are also required. Five to seven times during the quarter, experienced classroom teachers come to campus to model for students those strategies for teaching language arts skills which they have found to be most effective in teaching their own students. In addition, the "Reading and Writing Workshop" is taught by two professors so that teaming is effectively modeled during each class period. Then, later in the quarter, students observe in middle-level language arts classrooms and teach, in teams of two or three members, a mini-lesson to middle schoolers. Thus, our students are not "told" the importance of teaming; they experience that importance firsthand after seeing it modeled. These mini-lessons also give some of our students their first opportunity to work with adolescents from diverse backgrounds and experiences in authentic classroom settings. Thus, this particular assignment is also tied to Program Outcome I: Diagnoses Learning Needs.

In addition to the teaching experience in the middle school—one of the major assessment pieces of the course—and various lessons and projects created and taught to classmates, language arts students also create their own instructional materials and criteria for assessing their lessons and projects. For example, when studying the writing process, students create a peer-editing checklist and both a holistic and criteria-based scoring guide by which their classmates assess their writing samples. When teaching classmates or middle-level learners, each teacher education student's instructional presentation is videotaped and later self-assessed using the CCSU speaking criteria. Also, after each presentation, students reflect upon the experience in their journals. The journal is a powerful self-assessment tool, for through reflection upon each experience, students can analyze it, offer ways to change the activity to more effectively suit a specific group of middle-level students, and understand why a lesson may or may not have worked. As they become more comfortable with self-assessment, they reach higher levels of understanding as they make connections and synthesize those connections with their previous learning. Many of our students include entries from their journals in their program portfolios as evidence of their growth over the two years.

When language arts students move to the next course in the series, they experience similar assessment practices. A major assessment in "Language Arts/Reading: A Literature-based Integrated Approach" is an interdisciplinary unit which students create in four- or five-member teams. All four modes of communication (reading, writing, speaking, and listening) are incorporated, appropriate trade books and other information sources are chosen (with an attached rationale), and activities for each content discipline are described, including exploratory subjects such as music, art, physical fitness, and technology. In "English 414: Adolescent Literature," each individual creates a "literary web" based on an adolescent novel, after seeing a web modeled for the group during the junior year. (A literary web is an interdisciplinary unit centered around one specific novel, short story, play, or other writing.) The language arts majors will actually teach their webs during their full-time internships. Consequently, students move from experiencing a model web to creating a web to teaching a novel using a web they have created. Such involvement with subject matter and integration of pedagogy throughout the junior year give our language arts majors and minors the best possible learning environment, not only for establishing a foundation in content, but also for implementing that content in their own teaching by using developmentally appropriate strategies for adolescents.

Conclusion

With the Teacher Education Program Outcomes as a foundation, course outcomes can be developed to contribute to the achievement of those outcomes. Assessment of program outcomes should not only measure students' understanding of course content but should also increase that understanding as well as their understanding of the assessment process and appropriate assessment techniques.

When assessment is defined as learning, a collaborative partnership exists between faculty and student. In this partnership, students as learners have to ask questions of themselves rather than just answer questions asked by someone else. Learners have to ask where they want to go in their learning and how they plan to get there. Faculty guidance in this collaborative partnership assists students in asking and answering questions such as, "What is it I now know? Where do I want to go? How am I going to get there?" In addition to asking their own questions, learners must reflect on what they know and how this knowledge can be used to accomplish goals. When assessment and learning are related, students have the opportunity to demonstrate what they know and can do.

■

References

Abbott, E. A. (1992). *Flatland: A romance of many dimensions.* New York: Dover. (Original work published 1884)

Foster, H. M. (1994). *Crossing over: Whole language for secondary English teachers.* New York: Harcourt Brace.

Jackiw, N. (1995). The Geometer's Sketchpad (Version 3.0) [Computer software]. Berkeley, CA: Key Curriculum Press, Inc.

Maxwell, R. J. & Meiser, M. J. (1997). *Teaching English in middle and secondary schools* (2nd ed.). Upper Saddle River, NJ: Merrill.

National Council of Teachers of English and International Reading Association. (1994). *Standards for the assessment of reading and writing.* Urbana, IL: Author.

National Council of Teachers of English. (1996). *Standards for the English language arts.* Urbana, IL: Author.

Structures Which Support
Changing Processes and Outcomes
in Teacher Education

■

Harvey Rude

W ishful thinking and legislation have poor records as tools for social betterment," according to Michael Fullan and Mathew Miles (1992). This statement is an appropriate summary of how the faculty at the University of Northern Colorado felt when provided with a legislative mandate (H.B. 86-1187) to become "Colorado's primary institution for graduate and undergraduate teacher education" in 1986. A set of high expectations was cultivated as a result of this mandate to increase the effectiveness of a reputable teacher education program in a university of approximately 10,500 students. The institution has a rich history of commitment to the preparation of future teachers through its roots as the state's "normal school," and thus, the university community rallied around this challenge for future growth, development, and focus on improvement of its teacher preparation initiatives.

The University of Northern Colorado (UNC) has made commitments to develop better means of preparing future teachers through strong faculty ownership of integrated programs based on a philosophy of reflective practice. This paper provides an overview of the significant innovations that have been developed within these newly developed programs which are known as Professional Teacher Education Programs (PTEPs).

Each PTEP focuses on four major areas:

- integrated/coherent program content;
- professional development school approaches to program delivery;
- accountability through program standards and performance assessment; and
- the organizational process of systemic change.

As the programs are described in detail, an analysis of problems encountered, opportunities embraced, and future momentum has been provided.

Integrated/Coherent Program Content

Over the course of a three-year period, the faculty at the University of Northern Colorado were provided with a clean slate upon which to create totally different and unique programs. All faculty involved in teacher preparation received a charge from the college dean to invent the best possible teacher education programs. In response, the teacher education faculty developed four distinct Professional Teacher Education Programs (PTEPs) that addressed the needs of educators in the elementary, middle grades, high school, and P–12 specialist (art, music, physical education, and special education) areas. The integrated and sequential program content which emerged through the lengthy process of program development was extremely important as a foundation for identifying the standards that were unique to each of the four PTEPs. Without coherent and specific description of program content at the different levels, it would be close to impossible to assess the impact of the new programs on the development of future teachers. As Galluzzo and Pankratz (1990) have pointed out, the explication of teacher education program "knowledge bases" serves as an essential foundation for identification of what is distinctive about the preparation of educators.

As UNC moved from a "one-size-fits-all" version of its teacher education program to four distinct versions, with unique knowledge bases for four different programs, the university's governance processes did not embrace the innovations presented by the new design. As Hall and Hord (1986) have summarized the phenomenon of change in educational organizations, "change is a process and not an event." The process of curriculum approval of the programs, from final submission by the program faculty until official approval was granted by the Undergraduate Council, ground down the faculty authors through an interminable set of delays lasting nearly two years.

By the time the programs were officially approved, most faculty were convinced that the new programs would never receive approval, and resigned themselves to continuing the previous program. This slow start tempered the momentum which would be needed for implementation. The initial enthusiasm generated by the programs' invention needed to be rekindled in the inventors. The challenges of expanding program ownership to teachers and principals in partner schools provided the spark.

Professional Development Schools (Partner Schools and the National Network for Educational Renewal)

Collaboration has been defined by skeptics as "an unnatural act performed by unwilling participants." A major shift in the thinking of the UNC teacher education faculty was to cultivate a professional development school model of program delivery. As a member institution in John Goodlad's National Network for Educational Renewal, UNC was well poised to develop a significant agenda for simultaneous renewal of schools and university teacher education through congruence with Goodlad's (1994) four functions of partner schools:

1. preparing aspiring teachers and other educators
2. continuing education for professionals
3. conducting inquiry; and
4. providing an exemplary education for all students.

The partner school innovation provided extensive access to authentic settings which would become critical to support authentic assessment of teacher candidates.

An important element in the success of partner school arrangements is the extent to which the intended outcomes of the teacher preparation programs can be communicated with precision to cooperating teachers at the P–12 level. The benefit of well-articulated program standards makes clear the shared purposes of the collaborative work between the teacher education program and the partner school. Without clearly defined standards and a basis for assessing the degree to which teacher candidates are attaining these standards, the potential for simultaneous renewal of both entities in the partnership is severely limited. Simultaneous renewal includes an emphasis on shared responsibility between higher education and P–12 educational systems for a continuous system which ensures that all children can learn and achieve their own individually configured excellence (Rude, 1997).

A major benefit of UNC's partner school relationships has been the ongoing involvement of partner school teachers in the delineation of program standards and criteria for expected levels of performance. An interesting benefit that emerged was that unique perspectives from both university and partner school educators which have resulted in a rich set of program standards and expected levels of proficiency in teacher candidates. To make these innovations effective and accountable, a systematic approach was needed for assessing and documenting student and program efficacy. The final piece of the restructuring puzzle fell into place with UNC's participation in the Alverno College *Teaching for Tomorrow* Project.

Standards and Performance Assessment (Alverno College's *Teaching for Tomorrow* Project)

While the process of identifying the program standards for each PTEP was a convenient starting place for the implementation of the new programs, the most significant challenge for the PTEPs was the identification of authentic assessment approaches and strategies. The rationale for developing such a process was to provide a meaningful mechanism for feedback to prospective teachers in the pipeline. Many faculty viewed the potential commitment to such an assessment approach with skepticism based on concerns about inadequate time to manage such a system. By taking small steps to identify an authentic approach to assessing program outcomes, each PTEP was provided with the necessary autonomy and latitude to create its own assessment plan.

The impact of technical assistance was a credible source of support to faculty participants in PTEP design. The availability of experienced Alverno College faculty to work with the various PTEP faculty groups in designing authentic assessment plans has been invaluable. The "what" of program content coupled with the "how" of partner school implementation was complemented by the "how do you know" innovation of performance assessment. The importance of this final innovation was not initially appreciated by the faculty who had created the sequential and coherent programs of professional teacher preparation. The emphasis on faculty ownership for this effort was developed in a manner that provided a leadership role for all interested participants. As Kouzes and Posner (1987) view this phenomenon, leadership is not a private preserve of a few charismatic women and men, but rather a learnable set of practices that virtually anyone can master.

As the trials and tribulations of creating the best programs have crashed into the pragmatic world of practice, the philosophy and practice of program assessment has become a useful barometer for determining the focus for teaching and learning. Faculty were initially frustrated by an inability to teach all desired content in a given course due to the constraints imposed by course integration, available time, and team teaching. What helped to resolve this dilemma was the cultivation of an ongoing process of academic discourse and consensus with colleagues on what will be taught. The success of these negotiations was due to an emphasis on the "big understandings" which teacher candidates should develop from a particular course or experience. From a content perspective, "less is definitely more" with respect to developing the necessary knowledge, performances, and dispositions of teacher candidates.

Throughout the process of changing the structure, culture, and timing of the teacher preparation programs, a variety of challenges have been met. As with all innovations, it is tempting to blame everything on the new program. For example, enrollments in the undergraduate programs experienced a slight decline in the first year of PTEP implementation. The rallying cry from voices across the institution was that "the PTEPs are responsible for losing student enrollments." H. L. Mencken was right on target when he said, "For every complex problem there is a simple solution, and it is wrong." The final section provides some insights into our learning in the process and implementation of program change at the University of Northern Colorado.

The Process of Change (Leadership and Implementation)

A significant challenge which accompanies the process of change is the difficulty of maintaining focus in the ever-increasing complexity and chaos which define systems. Fullan (1994) identifies the key elements that must be addressed in the process of successfully negotiating change as the three Rs of restructuring, reculturing, and retiming. The restructuring which has occurred in UNC's College of Education is a direct result of the integrated program development through PTEPs. As the PTEPs were being finalized, the college was reorganized in fall 1994 to create a new structure called the School for the Study of Teaching and Teacher Education. The purpose of this new school-within-a-college was to provide an

---

ongoing forum for convening conversations about teaching and teacher education (Galluzzo, 1994).

While changes in structure can foster support for innovation and restructuring of teacher education, changes in culture and timing are more difficult. Nurturing a climate of mutual support across various professional disciplines, extending to the arts and sciences faculty and P–12 educators, has proved to be a monumental task. To dramatically change this dynamic, a commitment to re-timing or finding mutual times for collaboration and planning became critical, as well as sharing priorities as accurately and openly as possible. Expressing and extending these priorities was best accomplished by trusting the motivation and values of faculty members who will act in the best interest of the teacher candidates.

The "lessons we are learning" include:

Program Ownership. The hardest part of commitment to performance assessment-based programs is the recognition that the program is greater than the sum of the individual faculty. If an essential element of a program does not initially match with an individual's priority, it is predictable that the individual will ask, "Whose program is this? That wasn't my idea." This concern becomes a legitimate issue for building creative tension (Senge, 1990) in support of the faculty's role as being responsible for the curriculum and programs of the university.

We Don't Have the Time. Moving from a teacher education program that was heavily focused on process to one that values outcomes produces new demands for how faculty and staff will spend their time. To think in terms of adding responsibilities to an already full plate will only cultivate frustration, stress, and lack of effectiveness. Rethinking how time is committed to support the big ideas of the programs reinforces the value of supporting the essential functions of integrated content, partner schools, and performance assessment. The basic premise that time is a constant (there is no more time to borrow from the bank) requires that priority be given to those activities which support or enhance program outcomes.

The State Agency Won't Let Us Do This. The imaginary "ogres" will continue to stalk innovations that emerge around the world, regardless of the profession. In teacher education programs, the major culprits are typically the State Education Agency and the State Commission on Higher Education. In addressing the concerns of regulatory agencies, the guiding philosophy that works best is to use bureaucracy as leverage for positive change rather than an obstacle to progress.

Value for Collaboration and Teaming. "I would have finished this sooner, but I had help," is a frequent lament of parents who cook with their young children and teacher educators working in collaborative programs. The value of collaborative teams is that significant outcomes for teacher candidates are developed from a viewpoint which includes sufficient breadth and depth. Finding the time for collaboration with colleagues is well worth the investment. As faculty become more skillful in the process of collaboration, their involvement in the collaborative team approaches become more efficient and effective (Larson and LaFasto, 1989).

Academic Freedom. Standards and performance assessments are often viewed as constraints which stifle autonomy and the flexibility to determine what is taught in teacher education programs. Nothing could be farther from the truth when the outcomes for programs and courses become clearly specified. With accurate and ongoing assessment information provided to teacher candidates, the determination of how the outcomes are achieved can represent unlimited possibilities. The advantage to teacher candidates is to know the expectations for proficiency in knowledge, performances, and dispositions from a program's entrance to exit. The advantage to faculty is that data on candidates' achievement is grist for more collaborative, as opposed to solitary and isolated, refining of program content.

No Time for Research. One of the great holy wars in higher education has been the ongoing debate over whether teaching or research carries a higher value (Affleck and Lowenbraun, 1995). As a Doctoral I institution, UNC has the unique advantage of supporting innovative programs for the initial preparation of educators and high-quality graduate programs. With the development of the PTEPs, several concerns have been raised about the "resource drain" which results from the labor-intensive models of initial teacher preparation. The biggest concern is that such a model will debilitate faculty research and publication requirements necessary to function as an effective graduate faculty member. While this continues to be an issue of concern, the most promising strategy to address the issue is to align programs of scholarly activity with the work of the PTEPs. The new programs provide a rich set of possibilities for focused inquiry and scholarship within the partner schools. Teachers at the school sites have demonstrated considerable interest and willingness to be involved in this research.

Metric for Determining Faculty Workload. When one describes the customary faculty teaching load in a given week to "civilians" who are not part of the university culture, a predictable reaction might be, "That's a good *day's* work!" This statement is based on the parameter which establishes nine hours of teaching each week for graduate faculty members and 12 for undergraduate faculty members. Program restructuring requires that we consider the actual time that is required in an average week to include supervision, assessment, collaboration, and travel time in addition to the responsibility for teaching and preparation. A different metric is needed which describes these responsibilities with more accuracy than the assigned course credits (Frazier, 1993). For PTEP faculty, the assignment of a three-credit-hour course has been redefined at the program level as nine hours devoted to a partner school each week. The Colorado Commission on Higher Education is exploring the possibility of providing differential faculty load credit for engagement in partner school work. It would be helpful to develop similar differentials for faculty engaged in performance assessment activities.

Insufficient Resources (materials, supplies, money, and assistance) To Do the Job. Implementing any innovation can be extremely resource intensive. When new responsibilities such as performance assessments are added to the full-time jobs of teacher education faculty, different resources will be required to support the new roles. Rather than prescribing the resources that are provided, the UNC leadership took a position which asked programs to identify what was needed to get the job done. All requests for additional resources to implement the PTEPs have been satisfied since the inception of the programs. Resources are being deployed in creative directions that support such areas as team planning, assessment, professional development, and inquiry.

Blame It on the Innovation. It is easy for an innovation to become the scapegoat and/or target for assigning blame when things do not go well (Pogrow, 1996). If the scheduling of classrooms and conference rooms results in glitches which inconvenience faculty or students, it is common at UNC to hear, "The PTEPs must have messed up our system." Implementing any change within the higher education arena requires a long view of outcomes and benefits. With the passage of time, we are hearing less about how the PTEPs are making life difficult for the university community, and more about the benefits resulting from the improved programs.

Reward Structures. One of the paradoxes of higher education is the fierce competition which takes place for rewards that are meager. Reward structures in universities have traditionally focused on products related to the three-part faculty role of teaching, research, and professional service.

To effectively support the program components of the PTEPs, the College of Education is working on redefining the faculty evaluation system. The guiding principle behind this work is to align the system which rewards faculty through evaluation, promotion, tenure, sabbatical leave, travel, released time, and merit pay with the values placed on integrated programs, partner schools, and performance assessment.

Clash of School and University Cultures. When confronted with an innovative idea that is working extremely well within the pragmatic world of practice in schools, the stereotypical response from "insufferable academics" who populate teacher education programs in higher education is akin to, "That's all well and good, but will it work in theory?" The cultures of P–12 schools and universities are unique and not necessarily reciprocal. To be truly authentic, assessment practices must secure meaningful feedback about the effectiveness of teacher education programs from both school-based and university-based educators (Kaplan and Edelfelt, 1996).

As each PTEP evolved from a concept to a set of practices, the investment of time from P–12 and university faculty to build team structures and ownership for the programs has cultivated a relationship of trust and mutual respect. While organizational cultures will continue to differ, the understanding and commitment to support one another's organizational missions will foster effective collaboration.

In closing, the innovations represented by UNC's teacher education programs are clearly a work in progress. The combination of integrated, sequential, and coherent program content paired with significant investments in professional development school practices are held together through the commitment to well-defined program standards and assessments. As the faculty who invented the programs have embarked upon the journey of implementation, the rewards and successes have been matched with equal doses of dilemmas and challenges. As the artists and scientists among the faculty have received significant encouragement to go forth and do good work, unique and highly complex questions continue to emerge. The most striking impact of these efforts has been changes in the approaches to teaching by university professors. With the accountability of program standards and assessments, their instruction is more focused and driven by a commitment to achieve the desired outcomes for teacher candidates. A tremendous concern for the knowledge, skills, and dispositions to be acquired by the preservice student has modified the content and processes delivered by the faculty. The adage that "less is more" is an apt summary for the philosophy of teacher educators who are seeking to facilitate these outcomes for their students.

To maintain dynamic and creative tension as leverage for the positive growth of the programs, strategies which value faculty and promote their professional development have become a top priority. As Covey (1989) suggests, highly effective people begin with the end in mind resulting in two creations of their most important work. The first creation relies heavily on creativity, leadership, and vision to identify priorities from an unlimited set of possibilities. (When everything is a priority, nothing is a priority.) The second creation is based on the individual's capacity to put first things first, and execute these priorities in a manner that is highly efficacious. The necessary balance of the two creations is an ongoing challenge for our work. In the midst of all these changes, the reliance on program standards and assessment have provided a useful yardstick for the achievement of our priorities.

As the programs achieve a reasonable measure of consistency and predictability, the commitment to institutionalize the resources which support the various innovations is critical. Institutionalization can take a number of different expressions, including load credit for performance assessment responsibilities, faculty rewards that are based on the attainment of learner outcomes, and expansion of the focus on program standards and assessments beyond the teacher education program at the institution. The stage has been set for attainment of these outcomes, and the teacher education programs provide a useful set of resources to achieve the broader level of institutional impact in the future.

References

Affleck, J. & Lowenbraun, S. (1995). Managing change in a research university special education department. *Teacher Education and Special Education, 18*(2), 77-83.

Colorado Commission on Higher Education. (1986). House Bill 1187: The Role and Mission of Colorado Public Colleges and Universities. Denver, CO: Author.

Covey, S. (1989). *The seven habits of highly effective people.* New York: Simon and Shuster.

Frazier, C. (1993). A shared vision: Policy recommendations for linking teacher education to school reform. Denver, CO: Education Commission of the States.

Fullan, M. & Miles, M. (1992). Getting reform right: What works and what doesn't. *Phi Delta Kappan, 73*(10), 744-752.

Fullan, M. (1994). *Change forces: Probing the depths of educational reform.* Bristol, PA: Falmer Press.

Galluzzo, G. (1994). A plan for the reorganization of the College of Education at the University of Northern Colorado. White paper prepared for the faculty of the college.

Galluzzo, G. & Pankratz, R. (1990). Five attributes of a teacher education knowledge base. *Journal of Teacher Education, 41*(4), 7-14.

Goodlad, J. (1994). *Educational renewal: Better teachers, better schools.* San Francisco, CA: Jossey-Bass.

Hall, G. & Hord, S. (1986). *Change in schools: Facilitating the process.* Albany, NY: State University of New York Press.

Kaplan, L. & Edelfelt, R. (1996). (Eds.). *Teachers for the new millennium: Aligning teacher development, national goals, and high standards for all students.* Thousand Oaks, CA: Corwin Press.

Kouzes J. & Posner, B. (1987). *The leadership challenge: How to get extraordinary things done in organizations.* San Francisco, CA: Jossey-Bass.

Larson, C. & LaFasto, F. (1989). *Teamwork: What must go right/what can go wrong.* Newbury Park, CA: Sage.

Pogrow, S. (1996). Reforming the wannabe reformers: Why education reforms almost always end up making things worse. *Phi Delta Kappan, 77*(10), 656-663.

Rude, H. (1997). Professional licensure of educators. In J. Paul *et al.* (Eds.), *Special Education Practice.* Pacific Grove, CA: Brooks/Cole.

Senge, P. (1990). *The fifth discipline: The art and practice of the learning organization.* New York: Doubleday.

The Development of a Standards-Based Assessment Plan in a School-University Partnership

Mary Heuwinkel and Patricia J. Hagerty

A t the University of Northern Colorado, the task of designing a standards-based assessment plan for the newly developed Elementary Professional Teacher Education Program (PTEP) became both an end and a means to an end. As elementary teachers in partner schools collaborated with university faculty to write outcomes and rubrics, establish benchmarks, and create course and program assessments through which preservice teachers could demonstrate their competencies, the emerging school-university partnership both facilitated the process and became a product of it. This is a story of simultaneous renewal centered on the development of standards-based assessment.

Understanding the Context

The Elementary Professional Teacher Education Program

The Elementary Professional Teacher Education Program (PTEP), designed over a course of six years, was fully implemented in fall 1996 after a pilot year. Following the principles of Goodlad's National Network for Educational Renewal, the PTEP is based in partner schools,

---

with the goal being simultaneous renewal of schooling and the education of educators. The partner schools and UNC seek to accomplish four purposes:

1. Prepare teachers;
2. Provide professional development for educators;
3. Conduct inquiry;
4. Provide an exemplary education for all students.

The Elementary PTEP is spread across five semesters. The sophomore-level Seminar I has coursework that includes educational foundations, multiculturalism, school law, and educational technology. Seminar II includes coursework in educational psychology and in teaching exceptional learners. The junior-level Seminar III is the first site-based course and is taught at a partner school. Students are immersed in the life of an elementary teacher as they learn about classroom management, standards-based teaching, models of teaching, and the principles of a democratic classroom. Seminar IV is a semester-long integrated methods course, while Seminar V, also a semester long, includes a second integrated methods course as well as student teaching. During this last semester, the integrated methods course lasts five weeks and student teaching takes place during the last ten weeks.

Students are placed in a partner school in cohort groups of 20-25, where they stay for Seminars III, IV, and V. In a few cases, students leave their partner schools to student teach, but this is the exception rather than the rule.

Development of the Standards-Based Assessment Plan

The development of a standards-based assessment plan for the elementary program was initially motivated by two major forces: (a) the adoption of standards for teacher licensure at the state level and the concomitant requirement of teacher education programs to demonstrate how they were preparing preservice teachers to meet those standards; and (b) movement at the university level towards standards-based assessment of all students. Two key resources, a graduate assistant employed specifically for the project and participation in the *Teaching for Tomorrow* Project with Alverno College, further stimulated this work. Additionally, the re-formation of the teacher education program provided an entree for this revolutionary approach to assessing, and therefore teaching, preservice students.

In fall 1995, then, besides piloting the new program at two elementary schools, the Elementary PTEP faculty began the process of conceptualizing the standards-based assessment plan. In an effort to bring the school and university faculties together as true partners, an Elementary PTEP assessment committee was formed that included four teachers from each of the two initial partner schools. University faculty on the committee included instructors from educational psychology, special education, educational technology, foundations, and elementary methods courses as well as representatives from arts and sciences and health and human services. Using subcommittees to draft prototype documents for revision by the larger committee, this assessment committee adopted six program outcomes, detailing knowledge, performances, and dispositions for each (see Table 1). After establishing the benchmarks, a subcommittee developed rubrics for each outcome which listed the criteria to be met by each benchmark. By the end of the 1995–96 academic year, discussion of the program portfolio and course and program assessment tasks was underway. Meanwhile, another subcommittee had drafted a proposal for the criteria and tasks to be used for a two-stage marked entry process.

During fall 1996, faculty focus was on full implementation of the PTEP program in partner schools. Assessment work was put "on hold" except for development of the second stage of the marked entry process, which was done by only the faculty who taught the methods courses. Partner school faculty were only involved in the actual marked entry events, collaborating as equal partners in the selection of preservice teachers for continuation in the program. Meanwhile, two faculty members implemented the outcomes by using them as the foundation for their courses.

In January 1997, assessment work began again as the Elementary PTEP assessment committee, including representatives from the new partner schools, met in a one-day retreat. The focus was on designing in-course assessments and developing the purpose and structure of the program portfolio. In succeeding weeks, revision of the marked entry process was considered.

The first year of assessment work, 1995–96, had been one of conceptualization of standards-based assessment in higher education in general and particularly of an assessment plan for this teacher education program. Much of this work was done by a few university faculty members and the teachers from the partner schools. Although attendance at initial assessment meetings was high, university faculty became less involved during the year, for several reasons which will be explored later in this chapter. One of the major reasons was faculty preoccupation with full implementation of the new program in the following fall.

Table 1. Program Outcomes for the Elementary Professional Teacher Education Program

---

UNIVERSITY OF NORTHERN COLORADO
OUTCOMES FOR THE ELEMENTARY
PROFESSIONAL TEACHER EDUCATION PROGRAM

MISSION STATEMENT: The mission of the Elementary Education Professional Teacher Education Program is to prepare and empower proficient novice educators who are and will increasingly become reflective decision makers and practitioners.

Throughout the Elementary PTEP, teacher candidates will develop knowledge base, performances, and dispositions in the following areas:

1. Professionalism: The teacher candidate is a life-long learner who inquires, reflects, makes effective and appropriate decisions, and teaches to the democratic ideals of our diverse society.
2. Communication: The teacher candidate communicates effectively and professionally with students, their families, colleagues and other members of the diverse community.
3. Content Knowledge: The teacher candidate understands the nature of the disciplines and the content knowledge essential to promoting student construction and acquisition of new knowledge.
4. Instructional Techniques: The teacher candidate understands the learning process and applies strategies to effectively facilitate maximum learning for all students.
5. Learning Environment: The teacher candidate creates and maintains an environment that is accepting and intellectually challenging to all students.
6. Assessment: The teacher candidate uses a variety of assessment strategies and approaches to evaluate and improve teaching and learning in the classroom.

The second year, 1996–97, was initially conceived of as a year of implementation and refinement of the assessment plan, as well as of continued development. The decision was made to temporarily suspend this work for a semester, however, due to the intense effort required to implement the new program in partner schools. Therefore, during fall semester 1996, the Elementary PTEP assessment committee did not meet and partner faculty were not involved in assessment work except during marked entry events. Plans following the January retreat focused on continuing the development and implementation of the assessment plan in the spring with involvement from the entire assessment committee.

Interplay Between Assessment Plan Development and the Partnership

The Role of the Partnership in Development of the Plan

The collaboration between the university and partner school faculties in the development of the assessment plan was instrumental to the validity of the plan. Just as the vision of partner or professional development schools suggests (Goodlad, 1990, 1994; Holmes, 1990), joining the two faculties resulted in a blending of theory and practice. Elementary teachers brought a practical perspective and appropriate expectations for the performance of preservice teachers in the classroom, as well as "field-based language" more suitable for preservice teachers than university "jargon." University faculty brought theoretical frameworks of teacher knowledge and skills, reflecting current emphases such as cognitive learning theory, democratic ideals, reflection, and inquiry. The fact that both faculties had experience with preservice teachers at varying levels in the previous program ensured that the assessment plan provided for a progression in the development of knowledge and skills.

The sharing of school and university resources was also important. Because the elementary-level teachers were beginning to implement standards-based assessment in their classrooms, they had valuable conceptual and practical information to share with university faculty who had little training or experience in the area. District inservice training on standards-based assessment was open to university faculty, although the leap from designing specific elementary assessments to formulating an assessment plan for an entire teacher education program was a bit too wide for the experience to be of much help. University resources included funds from Goals 2000 grants and the university assessment committee, which were essential in providing substitutes for the elementary teachers. The facilitation by the Alverno consultants in the *Teaching for Tomorrow* Project was also instrumental in supporting the collaboration of the two faculties.

Finally, the congruence between the professional development school aspect of the program and standards-based assessment greatly facilitated development of the assessment plan. Because the program is built around experience in partner schools with an emphasis on learning for performance, a standards-based focus on demonstrating competencies fits naturally with the Elementary PTEP. This focus on performance, shared by school and university faculty, provided the common aim required for collaboration on the assessment project.

The Role of the Plan in Developing the Partnership

Just as the partnership facilitated development of the assessment plan, the work on the plan facilitated the development of the partnership. In their first year of work together, focusing together on a specific task was important to both faculties in developing an interdependent relationship. The task became the vehicle for the development of partnership for several reasons.

First, work on the assessment plan provided for each partner a glimpse of the other's culture, particularly of working norms. This understanding is critical to effective communication, including decision-making and problem-solving. Teachers became aware of the university norm for critical examination of information and ideas, while the university faculty became more sensitive to the value placed on consensus by the school faculty. As the year progressed, the P–12 teachers became more confident in expressing their ideas as they began to understand the university norms and realized that their opinions were being given serious consideration.

Second, the partnership was strengthened through joint ownership of the assessment plan. Each partner already had a vested interest in the growth of the preservice teachers, and collaborating on the plan allowed them to recognize that mutual concern and build upon it. This joint work also formalized each partner's role in assessing the preservice teachers. The Elementary PTEP had been designed largely by university faculty; now partner school faculty were intimately connected with the assessment aspect.

Finally, simultaneous renewal (Goodlad, 1990, 1994) of both faculties was begun through this focus on teaching competencies. School faculty found a new awareness of the complexity of teaching and learning to teach through close examination of the knowledge, skills, and dispositions outlined in the program outcomes. University faculty began to view teaching preservice teachers differently as they focused on their students' acquisition of knowledge and skills to perform as successful classroom teachers.

Effects of Implementation of the Assessment Plan

At this point, only a few Elementary PTEP faculty members have used the program outcomes and rubrics in their teaching at partner schools. The results have been positive. Faculty found that course topics that might once have been "near and dear" to the heart had to be deleted if they did not fit with program outcomes. All course topics now had to be correlated with program outcomes and key concepts within those outcomes. Assignments also had to be correlated with outcomes and key concepts. Faculty had to think creatively to develop assignments that addressed as many different outcomes and key concepts as possible, so that students were not overwhelmed by a large number of assignments.

The students in the program have also been affected positively by the initial use of the program outcomes and rubrics. They are able to see why a topic is included in a particular course and why a particular assignment is given. They can now see how a particular course, and its topics and assignments, fit into the larger Elementary PTEP. Students know "up front" what they will need to know to exit a seminar and the program. Students also understand that their professional portfolios need to be developed around the program outcomes and must include "artifacts" that represent their learning across outcomes.

Partner school faculty have also seen benefits in the implementation of the program outcomes and rubrics. They understand what the UNC students are expected to know after each seminar or set of courses. They also understand why a particular assignment has been given and can see its connection to program outcomes or key concepts. For example, partner school faculty can see the importance of the UNC students writing in journals to promote their reflection skills, since this journal writing is directly related to at least two program outcomes, Professionalism and Communication.

Partner school faculty have also been given the opportunity, at the end of Seminars III, IV, and V, to assess the UNC students on the progress they have made toward completing each of the program outcomes. To complete this assessment, the faculty must use the descriptors in the rubrics, which helps them see how the program is connected across courses.

The potential effects of implementation of the assessment plan are many. With a common focus by all university faculty members on the outcomes, more consistency is possible between sections of the same course. Similarly, with the rubrics as a guide to the development of knowledge and skills, greater coherence between courses can be achieved. The rubrics may also serve as the foundation for truly integrating methods courses now taught concurrently, which may increase collaboration among the colleges of education, arts and sciences, health and human services, and visual and performing arts. Standards-based assessment may be the linchpin in a cohesive, quality teacher education *program* instead of a collection of unrelated courses.

Insights into the Process

Many insights have been gained in the past 18 months of assessment work in the partnership. One lesson learned is that ownership and commitment are separate entities, both of which are required for implementation of the assessment plan. Ownership is possibly easier to achieve, even when joining P–12 and university faculties, if conscious attention is paid to the value of everyone's contributions. It grows through providing access to information, seeking and respecting all ideas and opinions, and facilitating group decisions at every turn. Ownership is a prerequisite for commitment, which appears to be more elusive in the higher education environment. Commitment requires establishing a common focus on the assessment plan so that individuals will choose to give it a high priority. In the highly autonomous and diverse culture of the university, creating this common focus is a challenge. Maintaining it is equally difficult, especially in a constructivist activity such as this where the outcome is unclear and the processes are evolving. At UNC, university faculty found it difficult to resist the pressure of phone messages, student and coursework concerns, and meetings on other matters to attend all-day meetings on assessment. P–12 faculty found this easier because they were on campus, further removed from their job demands, and heartened by their school's placement of a high priority on this work, as evidenced by releasing them from usual duties for the day.

A foundation of both ownership and commitment is a shared understanding of the basic principles of standards-based assessment. One such principle is that standards frame the courses instead of being an "add-on" to courses already designed. Faculty who do not grasp this essential point cannot own and be committed to implementing a standards-based curriculum and process. They must first understand the difference between it and the traditional curriculum and process. This tends to be a cart-and-horse proposition, because understanding such principles also requires a measure of experimentation with them. Thus we come to a third insight, the complementary nature of implementation and conceptualization.

Conceptualization and implementation inform one another. Particularly with a new venture such as designing a standards-based assessment plan, abstract conceptualization can only proceed for a limited time before ideas must be tested. Piloting foundational portions of the plan is critical because it surfaces unforeseen contingencies and issues that affect succeeding aspects of the plan. For example, the program portfolio developed in January is quite different from the one proposed a year earlier as faculty have begun to use portfolios. Since the portfolio is a major assessment device for the program, its structure affects other assessment tasks. The initial portfolio required the inclusion of specific assignments, which was intended to provide consistency between sections of the same course. The revised portfolio emphasizes student selection of "artifacts" that demonstrate meeting the outcomes. This portfolio allows faculty more freedom in designing assessment tasks while more strongly emphasizing that all course tasks must facilitate student learning toward the program outcomes.

Implementation also encourages ownership and commitment to the plan. Seeing for oneself the effects and the possibilities of the embryonic ideas as they are tested incites enthusiasm and a desire to revise and expand the original plan. Implementation also generates conversation around common progress and problems, which can ignite interest in faculty slower to adopt new practices.

A final insight is the contrast between the cultures of the two faculties. Small differences, such as norms for attending meetings and for conducting discussion, as well as underlying orientations towards action versus reflection, were illuminated by the collaboration on the assessment plan. Perhaps the most fundamental difference was in the perspective toward consensus. Partner school faculty were quick to reach consensus, while university faculty struggled with issues of academic freedom. A comfortable position on the continuum ranging from academic anarchy to capitulation is defined quite differently by the two faculties. This will likely be a major issue for some time to come.

Final Thoughts

As Fullan states in *Change Forces* (1993), change is characterized by unpredictability. The development of this standards-based assessment plan at the University of Northern Colorado is a case in point. Progression towards implementing standards has been nonlinear, with unexpected setbacks and unpredicted progress. Insights into how to direct each stage of the process have emerged along the way, often with 20-20 hindsight. As a model of strategic planning, it has been a failure. Yet unforeseen benefits have occurred as well. Faculty have more clarity about what to teach in each course, since program outcomes frame the courses. Faculty and students in the program are more assured that different sections of the same course include the same topics and assignments. Students and faculty know what a UNC teacher education student should be able to do by the end of the program.

Fullan reminds us that change is also dynamic, complex, and inseparable from elements of the context. Thus, it is not surprising that the process of developing standards has positively influenced and been influenced by both the partnership and the emerging teacher education program. What other unexpected connections await us as we continue this work? What progress and problems will arise from these three changes that are simultaneously evolving? It seems likely that the road ahead will be filled with as many bumps, benefits, and insights as the stretch behind us.

■

References

Fullan, M. (1993). *Change forces: Probing the depths of educational reform.* Bristol, PA: Falmer Press.

Goodlad, J. I. (1990). *Teachers for our nation's schools.* San Francisco: Jossey-Bass.

Goodlad, J. I. (1994). *Educational renewal: Better teachers, better schools.* San Francisco: Jossey-Bass.

The Holmes Group. (1990). *Tomorrow's schools: Principles for the design of professional development schools.* East Lansing, MI: Author.

WINSTON-SALEM STATE UNIVERSITY

Faculty Involvement in Outcomes Assessment to Improve Learning and Teaching: A Proactive Implementation Model

■

Merdis McCarter, Carolynn Berry, Ruby Burgess,
Shirley Manigault, and Subash Shah

Over the past few years, growing concern over the apparent lack of enduring student achievement has spurred higher education faculty to begin to examine ways in which instruction and assessment of instruction can be made more meaningful and aligned with the student's life beyond the university. The enduring question is, "Once students exit the university, will they be able to apply their knowledge, skills, and understandings to real-world contexts?" Many theorists and researchers believe that outcomes-based education and assessment is one answer for this educational dilemma. The following chapter is a description of one university's "work in progress" toward a paradigm shift that includes the idea of student assessment of learning outcomes as a means of improving learning and teaching.

Winston-Salem State University is a multi-purpose, multicultural, historically Black, public institution with an integrated faculty and a student enrollment of over 2,800, 75 percent of whom are African American. The primary mission of Winston-Salem State University is to offer quality educational programs at the baccalaureate level.

Approximately three years ago, Winston-Salem State University was selected to be part of a Philip Morris grant made to Alverno College (1994–96) to reform teacher education through the *Teaching for Tomorrow* Project. One focus of this grant was to involve liberal arts faculty in teacher education reform. Winston-Salem State University sent a team of three liberal arts department chairs, two education department chairs, and one education faculty member to Alverno College for two weeks to develop a plan to enhance teacher education through the cooperation and collaboration of liberal arts faculty and education faculty. The team decided that to improve its teacher education program, Winston-Salem State University needed to move towards outcomes assessment in all programs, promote cultural norms supportive of innovations, and re-examine the faculty evaluation system in terms of faculty roles in facilitating student learning outcomes.

The move towards outcomes assessment and the development of an assessment model for Winston-Salem State University had begun in 1988 when the university engaged in a self-study. At that time, the mission statement was revised, educational and institutional goals specified, and preliminary assessments plans for general education and major programs developed. A second stage of the process included the development of a General Education Core (40 hours) and core goals, in spring 1994.

Development of the Model

Conceptual Frameworks

The faculty team that visited Alverno College to study its assessment model began examining assumptions about education, students, teaching, and learning; sharing ideas about developing a shared vision and a common language; and discussing modes of assessment, evaluation criteria, and student performance—in the context of the university's mission and goals. We reviewed goals to identify abilities demonstrated by graduates and assessed by faculty. The question, "What should students be able to do with the knowledge and skills they have gained?" guided our discussions, and we listed behaviors, attitudes, and dispositions as well as knowledge and skills. The process triggered a good deal of discussion—we started, stopped, and started again, revising our list as we clarified our thinking. The diversity of our team worked for us as we shared ideas, experiences, and examples. We agreed, disagreed, compromised, and finally reached consensus, constantly sharing individual reservations and stopping for reality checks.

As we continued our discussions, we culled eight abilities or transferable skills of liberal learning from the university's published goals. The abilities selected by the team and later approved by the entire university faculty and administration are communication, problem-solving, critical thinking, intrapersonal skills, interpersonal skills, multicultural/pluralistic perspective, aesthetic response, and healthful living.

The team talked about ways of developing student outcomes. Team members were uncomfortable with models which suggest that the learning process is a linear one, and several members objected to the behaviorist terminology used so often. Thus, we struggled to find a conceptual framework which would capture the dynamism of the teaching/learning process and which would be developmental but not linear.

During the past three years (1994–97), the development of the model has been influenced by Alverno College's (1994) Student Assessment-as-Learning Model, by Richard Paul's (1993) critical thinking approach to learning, and by the King's College course-embedded assessment model (Farmer, 1988). Alverno College focuses on assessing the student's performance on multiple measures over time following the development of specified abilities and the use of explicit criteria. In Richard Paul's model, disciplinary reasoning is used as a means of understanding the content of the discipline. Tactics and structures are used to redesign instruction so that students learn how to reason through the content and to think in the discipline. King's College embeds pre- and post-assessments in existing courses; these are extracted from an existing assignment, graded, and used for course and program assessment.

The Learning Gyre

The framework which we adopted and adapted we termed the "Learning Gyre." We wanted to suggest the dynamics of change and development, of progression and regression—the idea that students might move up and down in the process, and of repetition of precise techniques to gain proficiency. The Learning Gyre with its upward and downward spiraling seemed an ideal framework, one that is cyclical, progressive, and regressive (responsive to variables and to interventions); integrated, profound, and expansive; involves movement, force, and stimuli; and allows for diversity of learners in terms of culture, age, gender, and learning styles.

Cultural Norms and Collegial Participation

Our next step was to develop a plan and devise a strategy for presenting our ideas to the university faculty and begin the arduous process of obtaining significant faculty involvement and creating a shared vision and common language. We realized that the shift to an outcomes-based learning model would necessarily involve "changing the culture" of the campus. Such a change, if possible at all, would occur very gradually and must involve all of the university constituencies—faculty, staff, students, alumni, representatives from the business and corporate sector, and other community leaders.

We recognized that the most difficult problem would involve changing the cultural norms of the faculty—expectations that shape attitudes and behaviors of individuals and groups. The faculty norms define and shape how a university's outcomes-based learning model may be implemented. Specific norms that promote innovative and proactive work are listed in Table 1.

Our team realized that affective factors (Etzioni, 1988) would shape the faculty's perceptions and impact the development of an outcomes-based learning model. Overall, our collective experience suggested that faculty members' transformational experiences would encompass one of the following six affective stages: denial, indifference, resistance, recognition, exploration, and commitment. Those in denial might believe that outcomes assessment would not work. Faculty in the indifference mode might remain passive and apathetic. Faculty members in the resistance stage might verbalize their opposition to outcomes assessment or use a series of blocking tactics. We were aware that a critical mass level is reached when faculty recognize the need for a change and become receptive to exploring different innovations. The last phase, commitment, would require proactive involvement in developing and implementing an innovation. This knowledge about the faculty and two major principles guided and continues to inform the teams' work. One principle is that developing students' abilities is the responsibility of the entire faculty; and the second principle is that it is important to allow time for faculty to internalize the meaning of reform in terms of their own professional development and work.

Table 1. Faculty Norms That Promote Innovative and Proactive Work

ORGANIZATIONAL CULTURE

A. Norms to Promote Creativity

1. Risk-Taking
- freedom to try things and fail or make mistakes
- allow discussion of "dumb" ideas
- failure may develop new insights
- challenge the status quo
- don't be blinded by the past
- willingness to focus beyond the short term
- expectation that change is part of your job
- positive attitudes about change
- view problems as opportunities

2. Rewards for Change
- ideas are valued
- respect for beginning and effectively implementing ideas
- build into the structure budgets, opportunities, resources, merit
- attention and support of administrators
- celebration of accomplishments
- suggestions are implemented
- encouragement

3. Openness
- open communication and sharing of information, ideas, and experiences
- listen better
- open access
- bright people, strong egos
- broad and critical thinking
- accept criticism
- don't be too sensitive
- continuous learning
- intellectual honesty
- expect and accept "constructive" conflict
- willing to consult others

B. Norms to Promote Implementation

1. Common Goals
- concern for the students, the major program, the department, and the university
- teamwork and accountability
- willingness to share the credit
- sense of ownership
- eliminate mixed messages
- manage interdependencies
- develop shared visions and a common direction on an ongoing basis
- build consensus
- mutual respect and trust
- value collegial participation

2. Autonomy
- decision-making responsibility for curriculum development and assessment of student performance
- freedom to act
- expectation of action
- belief that you can have an impact
- delegation
- intrinsic motivation is critical

3. Belief in Action
- don't be obsessed with precision
- emphasis on results
- meet your commitments in a timely manner
- value getting things done
- hard work is expected and appreciated
- empower students and faculty
- emphasis on quality
- eagerness to get things done
- cut through the bureaucracy
- drive to improve and contribute
- value problem-solving
- value cooperation and division of labor

Notes

1. The above paradigm on organizational culture is modified from the version first developed by Charles O'Reilly.
2. Reference: O'Reilly, C. (1995). Corporations, culture and commitment: Motivation and social control in organizations. In B. M. Staw (Ed.), *Psychological dimensions of organizational behavior* (2nd ed.), Englewood Cliffs: Prentice Hall.

Implementation Plan

The implementation plan contained five major strategies to obtain faculty involvement and commitment:

1. Establish a campuswide structure for faculty to discuss the effects of outcomes assessment on learning/teaching;
2. Use an incremental approach to change by building on existing teaching strategies in use by faculty;
3. Use existing departmental structures to operationalize learning outcomes (abilities) as they are defined and applied in each discipline;
4. Design a faculty evaluation system which emphasizes student learning; and
5. Use collegial participation to develop all models.

Student Assessment for Learning and Teaching (SALT) Project

Phase I of the plan called for forming interdisciplinary satellite groups to refine the list of abilities and define and describe their properties. This project component was designed to develop a common language so that faculty could begin the conversation about how student assessment for the improvement of learning might change the faculty approach to teaching. Team members selected 18 faculty members from several disciplines to serve as facilitators at the monthly interdisciplinary meetings.

At these monthly meetings, one Friday afternoon each month, each of the eight groups discussed and refined one ability and aspects of that ability. Each satellite group used professional literature and research related to their specific ability to further refine and clarify the definitions and descriptions of that ability. Group facilitators presented summaries of their work to their members and to the full faculty at the monthly faculty meetings. These summaries were refined each month to reflect input from the full faculty. To ensure cross-discipline and discipline-specific discussions, faculty kept their departments apprised of the progress of the satellite groups and the group informed of the work of the disciplines. Team members agreed that this process was critical to university-wide acceptance and implementation of the model. The process compelled the faculty to grapple with and understand the aspects, definitions, and different levels of performance relative to each ability. This, despite faculty's insistence that the team define, describe, and identify levels of performance for each ability!

For example, faculty in the problem-solving satellite group defined what was meant by problem-solving in mathematics, science, English, and other disciplines from an interdisciplinary standpoint. Satellite group members also discussed and shared teaching strategies and materials with the entire faculty. At the end of the project's first year, narratives describing the abilities were published in the handbook, *Student Assessment for Learning and Teaching at Winston-Salem State University* (McCarter & Manigault, 1995).

By the end of the first project year (spring 1995 semester), departments were discussing the abilities under development in their major programs and general education courses. It was clear that clarifying, defining, and identifying levels of performance for eight abilities simultaneously was a formidable task and that narrowing and focusing on one or two abilities and then gradually including the others over time would be the best procedure to follow for implementing all the abilities across the campus. In fact, the data submitted by departments at the end of the first year showed that some aspects of communication, problem solving, and critical thinking were in development and that several modes of assessment were in use. However, the team and the vice chancellor for academic affairs agreed to narrow the focus to the two abilities that cut across the curriculum: communication and critical thinking.

During the second year of the project, the second phase, the vice chancellor for academic affairs requested that each faculty integrate the development of some aspect of communication and critical thinking, explicitly and systematically, in each course. He voiced our belief that the development of these abilities was the responsibility of the entire faculty. Each department also was asked to provide an operational definition relative to its discipline for the two abilities. Professional development support was provided in workshops on redesigning courses and classroom assignments, communication, critical thinking, and course-embedded assessments.

During the second year, a critical factor in the success of the project was that faculty unassociated with the team but at the affective stages of recognition and exploration conducted many of the workshops on redesigning assignments and courses. They demonstrated how they were developing the abilities in their courses. Faculty from biology, English, mathematics, medical technology, music, physical education, political science, and psychology shared their ideas on designing assignments that would develop communication and critical thinking abilities in students. They also provided hands-on exercises to guide faculty through the steps of course redesign. Faculty were able to see how they could redesign assignments for their classes to fit the new abilities.

For example, a psychology professor presented a redesigned research paper assignment. He changed the assignment from requiring one paper at the end of the semester to three abstracts of all articles for the paper submitted at regular intervals, with an opportunity to turn in the first draft of the paper for feedback. This new procedure developed analytical and summarizing skills of students and provided instructor feedback prior to the final evaluation of the paper.

During the workshops, faculty also participated in exercises relating to instructional redesign. These activities provided some specifics about what changes might be made in teaching and how faculty might consider ways of modifying an existing assignment to develop one or more aspects of an ability. One of their major concerns, however, was how to provide multiple assessments which would involve many writing and analysis assignments for large numbers of students, and provide students with prompt, high-quality, precise, and helpful feedback.

A second factor in the success of the project was the structuring of workshops for small groups of faculty. This was done with the communication and critical thinking workshops presented by Lucy Cromwell, one of our Alverno consultants, and critical thinking workshops provided by Merdis McCarter and Shirley Manigault, team members. By focusing assessment activities around writing and critical thinking and emphasizing individual discipline-based courses, we were able to lower faculty resistance.

Once it became clear to faculty that outcomes assessment was here to stay, faculty then said that it was not possible to do all that had been suggested without sacrificing content and satisfactory performance on licensure exams. The critical thinking workshops, in which reasoning through the content was emphasized as a way to help students develop understanding of a discipline, enabled the team to demonstrate that both content and abilities could be covered and that the ability to communicate and to analyze would provide a concrete way for faculty to determine the extent to which students really understand content.

Finally, a third factor in the success of the project was the willingness of the team to adjust the implementation plan. Throughout the project, team members met regularly as a group, with the vice chancellor for academic affairs, and with facilitators to discuss strategies and plan programs for faculty involvement and commitment to outcomes assessment. Meetings with facilitators were held prior to each interdisciplinary satellite group session. Adjustments in implementation plans were always made based on input from team members, facilitators, faculty, and the administration.

Links Between Faculty Evaluation and Student Outcomes Assessment

While the outcomes-assessment model was being developed, we were designing a faculty evaluation system and establishing teaching awards which emphasized and rewarded those aspects of teaching, such as instructional design and delivery, that facilitated the improvement of student learning. Of particular importance to assessment for the improvement of student learning is instructional design. And the faculty evaluation system called for documentation of the processes and products that were used to develop student abilities as exhibited in each faculty member's instructional design for each course.

The workshops by colleagues gave all faculty an opportunity to see examples of how redesigned assignments developed students' analytical, communication, and problem-solving skills. This provided a tie-in to what was meant in the faculty evaluation system by instructional design. These presentations, given by faculty members who were not team members or facilitators, achieved an additional goal of reducing other faculty members' resistance to outcomes assessment.

As a university changes and moves towards a paradigm which is focused on student learning outcomes, it is very important that the faculty evaluation and reward system be consistent with the changes. When we were just beginning to develop the Student Assessment for Learning and Teaching model, another faculty committee had already spent three years working on a new faculty evaluation system, defining faculty roles and developing a draft evaluation system.

The faculty evaluation system attempted to make the evaluation as objective as possible by emphasizing the collection of multiple data from multiple sources which were then applied to a predetermined mathematical model. While the committee was developing our faculty evaluation system, the Board of Governors of the University of North Carolina System presented, through the president of the University System, some evaluation procedures which were to be applied to all faculty across the university system. These included peer review, student rating of instruction, peer observation of instruction of non-tenured faculty, and a documented emphasis on teaching in evaluation, promotion, and tenure decisions. These mandates were incorporated into our faculty evaluation system.

As we moved forward with refining the evaluation system and the SALT Project, we realized that our efforts to improve student learning could also be used to help faculty improve their teaching. Additionally, we realized that if faculty were going to buy into the SALT Project, they needed to be assured that their attempts to change their teaching would be supported and rewarded (see Table 1). The Faculty Evaluation Committee changed the objectives in the Faculty Evaluation Manual to include as the first objective "to develop a framework within which the faculty role can be effectively assessed in order to promote student achievement," thus focusing on the role of teaching in terms of student learning. The faculty evaluation system also was revised to include multiple authentic assessments, multiple opportunities for feedback, and an emphasis on improvement and creativity for faculty members, similar to the system being developed for students.

While the system does allow for flexibility by individual departments, some assessments are required for all faculty. These include student rating of classroom instruction by questionnaire, peer observation, department chair observation, a portfolio, and a course dossier which are reviewed by a content peer and the department chair. Feedback is obtained from a number of sources.

During the process of developing our faculty evaluation system, the most important thing we learned was that faculty evaluation must be based upon a philosophy and not on a single or a collection of evaluation instruments. Once the institution's beliefs about faculty evaluation and its projected accomplishments are clear, then it is much easier to develop or find instruments to gather the pertinent data. The Faculty Evaluation Committee decided that our system would be developmental, identify strengths and weaknesses, and help faculty improve their teaching in a positive, not punitive, atmosphere.

With both the SALT Project and the faculty evaluation system, we are focusing on how to best facilitate student learning. This requires that faculty have the opportunity to experiment with new teaching strategies and reflect on what they are learning about learning. We think that our faculty evaluation system can help with this process. First, faculty are not penalized for trying something new regardless of whether it did or did not work. In fact, when properly documented, the change process can be rewarded. This is in keeping with the proactive norms in Table 1. Secondly, faculty are encouraged to engage in self-reflection and self-assessment through use of a teaching portfolio and a course dossier. The teaching portfolio includes the faculty member's philosophy, discussion of how beliefs are translated into teaching methodology and assessment of students, and actual pieces of student work to illustrate how instruction affected learning. The course dossier directly ties course objectives to instructional activities, indicates what assessments will be given for each objective, and provides the criteria by which student performance will be judged. It also contains contextual information about the course including a discussion about how the objectives, teaching methodologies, and assessments changed based on the results of the student assessments.

Conclusions

We began by asking ourselves if assessment of student performance and outcomes was a valid measure of program quality, and how assessment of student performance and outcomes might enhance teaching and learning at Winston-Salem State University. We raised these questions while attending an assessment workshop at Alverno College. We deliberated, discussed, examined, and argued many issues as we investigated techniques to shift WSSU's institutional focus from assessing teaching inputs to assessing both student learning outcomes and faculty teaching roles, with emphasis on improvement. We identified eight abilities to be developed in all Winston-Salem State University graduates. The abilities were selected according to their alignment with and support of the university's mission and educational goals. We explicated the central assumptions of the Student Assessment for Learning and Teaching Project and designated activities that would occur during the two phases of the project's implementation.

We learned several lessons that may be useful to institutions planning to undertake outcomes assessment university-wide. These lessons fall into two categories: (1) strategies that promote proactive behavior and (2) structures that promote reforms.

In our meetings and workshops, we found that the six affective factors explained how the faculty processed and responded to the assessment information and analysis provided by their colleagues and the Alverno College consultants. We recognized that to implement effectively our outcomes-based assessment model, we needed a "critical mass" of the faculty to be situated at the affective stages of recognition and exploration. Thus, faculty participation became critical for curriculum change and faculty governance. Without proactive team leadership, administrative leadership, and faculty participation in the development of the performance-based learning model, the goals of learning-based assessments were in danger of displacement.

Moreover, through faculty meetings and workshops on assessment, some of the norms for innovation and proactive work listed in Table 1 became more evident. For effective development and implementation of the outcomes-based learning model, it is important that these norms are valued and supported by faculty and administrators. Without this critical support and reinforcement of these cultural norms, the goals of outcomes-based assessment are in danger of derailment though mechanistic implementation.

From our perspective, the critical mass for implementing the outcomes-based learning model will be reached when the majority of the faculty are at the affective stages of recognition and exploration. We found that at these particular stages, faculty members from different disciplines became proactive and agreed to present their respective assessment strategies to the faculty in various interdisciplinary workshops.

When faculty members are at the dominant affective stages of denial, indifference, and resistance, our experiences indicate that conducting workshops for small groups and using course-based models tend to lower faculty resistance to outcomes assessment. We found that by undertaking discipline-based assessment activities around writing and thinking abilities, we were able to lower the faculty resistance towards outcomes-based assessment and enhance the possibilities of obtaining grounded incremental changes in the curriculum.

We found that, when faced with resistance and fatigue, the administrative support, ambition, and scope of the project served as an incentive to continue the process. This could be seen in numerous ways: in the faculty time allocated to the effort, the quality of faculty work, the complex system being implemented, and the willingness and insistence of the administration to extend the project to encompass the entire university.

We found continuous evaluation with appropriate adjustments to be an integral component of the SALT Project and the faculty evaluation system. The research informed construction of the original Student Assessment for Learning and Teaching, and the faculty evaluation models (Alverno College, King's College, Richard Paul, and Raoul Arreola) have continued to be informed by the data produced by participating faculty. Throughout the three years of the project, we can see this through the original contexts that helped us to define the basic goals and make numerous, substantive changes in both of the two interrelated efforts. This effort affirmed our belief that a comprehensive commitment to student assessment and a faculty evaluation system that focuses on learning require ongoing information on how their many components are working together and progressing.

We found that faculty who gave time to reflection increased their instructional abilities and became more effective. Through regular reflection, real growth happened continuously. Faculty began paying attention to the setting and meeting of their instructional goals. They started paying attention to the quality and quantity of student engagement in the teaching/learning process. They began to examine their own teaching strategies and how they could be altered to be more effective. They began judging their effectiveness by student participation and learning outcomes.

The results of both the SALT Project and the new faculty evaluation system should help us document the improvement of teaching. As we better define student outcomes and can more consistently measure student performance, we will better be able to judge how teaching has influenced student accomplishments. Because we are focusing on course-embedded assessments for student outcomes which will include pre- and post-assessments, we will have some indication of what learning occurred in the classroom and how the teacher influenced that learning. While we feel that our work to date has been rewarding, we still have a long way to go. Other institutions planning to design and implement such a program should be aware of the time involved in doing so.

References

Alverno College Faculty. (1994). *Student assessment-as-learning at Alverno College*. Milwaukee, WI: Alverno Productions.

Arreola, R. A. (1988). *Handbook for developing a comprehensive faculty evaluation system*. Memphis, TN: Center for Educational Development and Assessment.

Etzioni, A. (1988). *The moral dimensions: Toward a new economics*. New York: The Free Press.

Farmer, D. W. (1988). *Enhancing student learning: Emphasizing essential programs*. Wilkes-Barre, PA: King's College.

McCarter, M. J. & Manigault, S. F. (1995). *Student assessment for learning and teaching at Winston-Salem State University*. Winston-Salem, NC: Winston-Salem State University.

O'Reilly, C. (1995). Corporations, culture and commitment: Motivation and social control in organizations. In B. M. Staw (Ed.), *Psychological dimensions of organizational behavior* (2nd ed.). Englewood Cliffs, NJ: Prentice Hall.

Paul, R. (1993). *Critical thinking: How to prepare students for a changing world*. Santa Rosa, CA: Foundation for Critical Thinking.

PART III

The Change Process: Lessons Learned

Introduction

Mary E. Diez

In the previous section, the stories from teacher education institutions illustrate what happened when these institutions took seriously the need to shift from a focus on teacher education as a collection of courses to teacher education as the development of the knowledge, abilities, and attitudes of teacher candidates. For many of these institutions, because of a focus on liberal arts as part of teacher education, this shift extended to arts and science courses as well.

In the Philip Morris *Teaching for Tomorrow* Project (1994–97), the Alverno faculty team made explicit four elements of the process necessary to develop a standards-based teacher education program:

1. Clarity of outcomes: What should the beginning teacher know and be able to do?
2. Coherent curriculum: How can teacher educators design classes and field experiences so that candidates develop the intended outcomes?
3. Performance assessment: How can teacher educators link assessment developmentally to the outcomes, embed assessment in courses and provide on-demand tasks, and include self-assessment as integral to the process?
4. Links with P–12 schools: How can teacher educators provide meaningful hands-on experiences; keep the outcomes, curriculum, and

assessment relevant; and support similar efforts to develop P–12 curriculum and assessment?

While the four elements constitute essentials for moving toward standards-based teacher education reform, these stories demonstrate that there is a great deal more involved as faculty work through the stages of restructuring the teacher education program. Shifting the focus from a predominantly teacher-directed information dissemination system to a student-centered process of development entailed changes in assumptions, relationships, and practice. The following sets of questions provide a way to approach these three areas of change.

Assumptions

- How can we look at the enterprise as different from what we've done and how we've done it in the past?
- What does a teacher need to know and be able to do? What implications are there for change in the answers to this question?
- What kind of student performance needs to be assessed? What implications are there for change in the answer to this question?
- Who is in charge of our program? How much are we responsible for, and how much responsibility rests with the institution as a whole, with the state department of public instruction, with subject area specialty organizations, with the practicing profession, with our students, with national accreditation bodies?
- Is departmental structure both necessary and sufficient?
- Can we trust our own experience? Do we test our experience by sharing it with colleagues in higher education and P–12? by examining it in the light of current research, and standards developed at the state or national level?

Relationships

- How can we most effectively share information about a vision and about our work?
- How can we learn to work together more effectively? with liberal arts faculty? within teacher education? with P–12 colleagues? with the larger profession?
- How can we build the interdependence necessary for creating a coherent curriculum, for ensuring support for our students developing through the experiences we provide?

- How can we build joint ownership of a program rather than individual ownership of courses and expertise?
- How can we see education in a broader perspective, as interactive with the larger society?

Practices

- How can we structure the kinds of ongoing supports needed to keep us thinking and adapting?
- How do we use time and other resources to maintain collaborative work?
- How do we reshape our concept of faculty workload?
- How can we integrate reflection on our practice as an integral part of practice, so as to uncover new issues and areas of growth?
- How can we integrate our focus on teaching with requirements for research?
- What kind of reward structures will place value on the kinds of work with students and with schools required for effective standards-based teacher education?

In Part III, Alverno faculty members draw upon our experiences with the *Teaching for Tomorrow* Project, as well as on the reflections of the seven teacher education institutions in Part II. These three chapters address the climate necessary to begin a change process, the supports needed to continue it, and the institutionalization required to sustain it over time.

Creating the Climate for Change

■

Mary E. Diez and Leona C. Truchan

What triggers awareness of the need for change? At its heart, change involves questioning the assumptions that guide our current practice. It is easy to perceive the way we currently do things as the only way they can be done. The power of current practice tends to act as a blinder that prevents new ideas from consideration or exploration. Connections that once were tenuous new ideas begin to have the force of rules or laws. Their power lies in our no longer questioning them.

Once we allow questioning to de-couple the connections, however, it is possible to brainstorm other possibilities, see new relationships, and build new connections where before there had only been discrete pieces. It takes a concerted effort to build a new framework that focuses and connects these formerly separate parts.

What sparks a willingness to engage in questioning our assumptions? Clearly something has to jar our comfort with the way things are, to provide the reason to question. For teacher education, there are multiple forces—both external and internal—offering the stimulus to question assumptions.

External forces

Public dissatisfaction with the *status quo* is a key stimulus, evident in the current public dialogue dealing with questions about the quality of teacher education, higher education, and P–12 education. From *A Na-*

tion at Risk (1983) to the National Commission's report on *What Matters Most: Teaching for America's Future* (1996), the call for change has been persistent.

Mandates from external agencies can also invite the questioning of assumptions. These, too, have been numerous in the past 15 years. For example, the redesign by the National Council for Accreditation of Teacher Education (NCATE) of the standards and processes of accreditation calls upon institutions to make explicit the conceptual frameworks guiding and the knowledge bases undergirding their teacher education programs. Redesign clearly challenges the assumption of many institutions that a program is, essentially, a collection of courses. As NCATE moves toward a focus on performance standards and performance assessment, the questioning of assumptions will go deeper.

Similarly, as organizations like the National Council of Teachers of Mathematics and the National Research Council of the American Academy for Arts and Sciences develop standards for content, performance, and teaching, they present opportunities for teacher preparation institutions to examine the implications inherent in these national standards. Because systemic initiatives supported through national funding are tied to these standards, higher education's understanding of the standards and their implications is necessary for full participation in these initiatives. In addition, these projects require evidence of higher education's collaborative work with P–12 schools, another opportunity for questioning old assumptions. Durden and Hunt, for example, illustrate this dialogue between teacher educators and P–12 teachers in the description of the outcomes' development for the middle school program at Clayton College & State University.

In many states, standards boards, departments of education, and departments of public instruction have raised questions about their own assumptions in recent years. These bodies, charged with the development of standards for teacher education and licensure, are changing their approaches to the oversight of teacher education. Rude identifies the impetus of the state mandate of the University of Northern Colorado as Colorado's primary institution for graduate and undergraduate teacher education. Lowe and Banker describe the impact of the Kentucky Education Reform Act in initiating systemic reform of both P–12 and teacher education. In both cases, the individual teacher education institution was faced with the challenge to its past identity in the demands of an outside mandate.

Models of programs—even those implicit in a set of standards—may at first appear to be all-or-nothing propositions. Faculty may treat them not as a stimulus to thinking, but as a map to the path they must take. Such a view can solidify resistance. As they began working with the *Teaching for Tomorrow* Project, the Alverno faculty consciously avoided the imposition of "the Alverno model" on other institutions; rather, they strove to assist the project schools to create models to fit their own environments.

External forces are often a necessary part of the stimulus for change, but they are rarely sufficient to effect real change. As Heuwinkel and Hagerty note, lasting change requires both ownership and commitment on the part of those engaging in change. Absent the involvement required for ownership and commitment, change is likely to be cosmetic at best, undertaken only to the degree that it will "keep them off our backs."

Lest we become too complacent about the openness to change that marks academe, we should recall a study of five discipline areas completed in 1991 (Association of American Colleges & Universities, 1991). Researchers reported that in a review of catalogs over the 50 years between 1940–1990, few changes were made in course offerings, with the lone exception of technology—this despite enormous changes in society in the same period!

Internal forces

Assumptions about "the way things are" can be challenged when personal or group dissatisfaction with the *status quo* leads to desire for change. Experiencing student criticism (verbally or in the form of transfers to other institutions), dealing with student failure to perform or to be hired, or sensing a disjunction between the needs of the schools and the focus of a program—all can suggest a re-examination of the assumptions underlying one's work in teacher education.

Sometimes changes in other aspects of the enterprise raise the questions—e.g., changes in enrollment (numbers of students or the background experiences of students), changes in purpose or organization (as when several departments are merged into a new college or school), or changes in administration at the institution or in the school, college, or department of education. As described by Nelms and Thomas, Clayton College & State University was mandated to initiate its first-ever teacher education program, involving liberal arts faculty in the design of a field-based middle school program. McCarter *et al.* chronicle the work of faculty at

Winston-Salem State University, whose starting point was rethinking both the core curriculum and the faculty evaluation process.

Disequilibrium

When external or internal forces (or a combination) stimulate questioning of assumptions, the result is disequilibrium, described as "pain" by Mihalevich and Carr at Central Missouri State University. Individual or institutional responses to disequilibrium are varied. Sometimes a kind of paralysis leads to denial and a quick return to the prior assumptions. But disequilibrium can also be a liberating experience.

In the examples of institutions engaged in standards-based reform, much of the disequilibrium relates to the awareness that teacher education candidates' experiences in a set of courses do not necessarily result in their acquisition of the knowledge, skills, and dispositions needed to work effectively with a wide range of learner needs. Questioning the old focus of a program as a collection of courses opened the door to looking at other conceptual frameworks for programs. In the *Teaching for Tomorrow* Project, that framework was specified in four aspects: clarity of outcomes, coherence of curriculum, performance assessment, and links with P–12 schools.

What overcomes resistance to change and the desire to keep the *status quo*? The teacher educators who describe their change processes in the preceding chapters, first of all, engaged the questions about their practice. They sought ideas from outside their own institutions, using, among other things, the standards documents of the National Board for Professional Teaching Standards, the Interstate New Teacher Assessment and Support Consortium, and NCATE, and in some cases new state standards. They linked with other institutions in state or national networks and in more informal connections. Often the sharing of their issues and questions revealed a common sense of the problems or even ideas for new directions.

The three *Teaching for Tomorrow* institutions (Clayton College & State University, the University of Northern Colorado, and Winston-Salem State University) began with attending the Student Assessment-as-Learning Workshop at Alverno College. McCarter *et al.* describe the power of time away from the institution together for engaging their questions and developing tentative ways to address them with colleagues when they returned to the Winston-Salem campus.

One critical factor in overcoming resistance to change is an awareness that what is being proposed is not an add-on, but a rethinking of the way we work. In much of higher education restructuring, as in P–12, when faculty perceive the change to be something added to what they already do, they find it an overbearing challenge. For example, as Diez and Hass argue, if faculty continue to see the program as a collection of courses, then standards and assessment will be an added burden rather than a way of rethinking the whole process of developing a teacher.

The University of Northern Colorado's development of a new organizational structure—the School for the Study of Teaching and Teacher Education—clearly signaled that their change process was a rethinking and not an add-on. Several of the institutions described the necessity of working in genuine partnership with P–12 school personnel, although as Heuwinkel and Hagerty point out, making collaboration an integral part of the working life of both cultures is a continuing challenge.

What stimulates and gives energy needed to begin? Clearly, change in an institution cannot be accomplished through the awareness and insight of one person. But it also does not demand that all parties move at the same rate to the same end. What is needed is the commitment of a core group of people interested in making improvement, who agree to work toward the development of a common vision. This group must be large enough to provide energy to move the vision forward and bring others into the process.

Who is involved in creating a climate for change does matter. Generally, effective change requires both bottom-up and top-down support. All of the institutions described in Part II had support from internal leaders, representing the institution as a whole or the school, college, or department of education. For example, at Central Missouri State University, the change in teacher education built on earlier efforts focused on continuous quality improvement across the institution. At Winston-Salem State University, the impetus for university-wide change began with teacher education, but quickly gained the support of liberal arts chairs and the vice chancellor for academic affairs. Ashland University's efforts began with a call from the dean of the School of Education as part of the preparation for NCATE reaccreditation.

In many cases, incentives from external agencies join with internal forces to create a climate for change. Across most of these institutions, NCATE accreditation and state mandates were factors in both sparking change and guiding its process. Three institutions, fortunate enough to be in states with Philip Morris Companies, successfully completed proposals to become part of Alverno's *Teaching for Tomorrow* Project, which provided consultation support described more fully in the introduction to this volume.

Finally, across those involved in creating the climate for change, communication and persistence emerge as important factors. Communication provides the means of "glimpsing the other's culture" (Heuwinkel & Hagerty), which is an important first step in acknowledging different perspectives than one's own. It also makes possible what Schnug and Shelly describe as "an honest, ongoing audit of talent, strengths, desires, and resources."

Mihalevich and Carr document the importance of persistence in overcoming the "Nay-Sayers," whose resistance to change can dampen initial efforts to engage in the necessary dialogue. Both Clayton College & State University and Winston-Salem State University worked on multiple fronts to maintain focus and attention to the change process. Across all of these teacher education institutions, persistence is one key factor in moving to the next step.

References

Association of American Colleges & Universities. (1991). *Liberal learning and the arts and sciences major: Reports from the fields.* Washington, DC: Author.

National Commission on Excellence in Education. (1983). *A nation at risk.* Washington, DC: U.S. Department of Education.

National Commission on Teaching & America's Future. (1996). *What matters most: Teaching for America's future.* New York: Author.

Supporting Change in
Teacher Education Institutions

■

Jacqueline M. Hass and Julie A. Stoffels

The stories in this volume, from both large and small teacher education institutions, testify to the arduous work of maintaining commitment to the change process once the initial plans are set in motion. In all cases, institutional relationships and processes were developed which support individuals and groups as they grapple with moving to a standards-based teacher education program. These relationships and processes do not translate into a laundry list of necessary elements, nor can they be used as a check-off list to determine if one is ready to take the next step. Rather, they are elements which are found operating in an atmosphere where change is viable and realizable.

Developing Relationships

The institutions represented in Part II made an initial and serious commitment to a collaborative enterprise, recognizing that the task of moving to a standards-based model was a complex and important endeavor, requiring the efforts of many individuals over a long period of time. In addition to a promise of time and space, the commitment also required investing a faculty with the knowledge and skills to work together effectively over a considerable period of time. Schnug and Shelly articulate this lengthy and recursive process clearly in their tale of "Mission: Possible," as do Mihalevich and Carr, writing about the change process at Central Missouri State University. In these cases and in the others in this volume, internal and external relationships had to be developed to assure a successful venture.

Internal Relationships

Institutions involved in teacher education reform develop internal relationships that facilitate their work in the change process. Critical to forming these relationships is time. At the most concrete level, all of them must find a way to arrange for sufficient time for the amount of work that must be done. Rude reminds us that the demands of the task are infinite but there are a finite number of hours in the day. Retreats and extended workshops are two of the ways in which institutions have dealt with the time constraints, but each story reminds us that time for working together must be carefully budgeted and judiciously protected if change is to be supported.

The teams from the *Teaching for Tomorrow* Project, including both teacher education faculty and arts and sciences faculty, shared an initial two-week learning experience, where they forged new alliances and engaged in the cross-disciplinary work that would need to continue if change was to be grounded within the institution. For the team from Clayton College & State University, this extended workshop provided the time and space to plan for the middle grades teacher education program which they would begin during the following fall semester. Working together, they refined their outcomes and began the iterative process of incorporating them into the teacher education curriculum. The team from Winston-Salem State University developed a conceptual model for their program and a plan for changing the cultural norms of the faculty to a student-focused, outcomes-based model. In these cases, extended time and the opportunity to forge relationships increased the productivity and provided the support needed to engage in the reform work. The importance of these elements is reinforced in the chapter by Mihalevich and Carr, who point out that, in spite of both time limitations and everyday job-related distractions, their institution persisted in the change process.

To sustain change, faculty who work together need to develop a means to engage in a healthy discourse. Schnug and Shelly recognize the importance of effective communication in the process of change and comment that they hope to see their type of professional communication become an expectation of performance, "as much a part of 'faculty load' as teaching and scholarship."

Because each institution has a unique way of working and a culture of its own, faculty understand and develop ways to work with these elements in their particular setting. For example, the team from Winston-Salem State University, in trying to bring about a shared vision and a common language for teacher education, addressed the issue of changing the cultural norms of faculty as a component of their plan. They recognized that it would take time and planning to garner faculty involvement and commitment, and they strategized for maximum effectiveness.

Another awareness of cultures occurred in the stories of the work at the University of Northern Colorado (UNC) with teams from higher education and P–12 faculty. Heuwinkel and Hagerty write about the difference in the foci and working norms of the P–12 teachers and the UNC faculty, and how it continues to be something with which they struggle. They remind us that coming to consensus is quite different for the two groups: "A comfortable position on the continuum ranging from academic anarchy to capitulation is defined quite differently by the two faculties." Creating a common focus and developing an appreciation for one another's organizational mission takes time and honest communication, and is both a requirement and a by-product of the serious collaborative effort.

Because reform efforts are longterm, institutions need to find ways to support continuing faculty as they struggle to stay fresh and committed, and also to assist new faculty as they become involved in the team's ongoing work. One way to deal with this is to conceptualize the work in stages or phases as the team from Asbury College did, so that faculty have a map of the total process and can identify the current focus. The input of new participants is often a stimulus for new perspectives, especially when moving toward a standards-based program is valued and mentoring new faculty in this process is respected work.

Equally helpful to institutions engaging in reform are structures to assist teams to reflect upon the anticipated changes and alternative models as they are being developed. The mechanisms vary by institution: sometimes there are regularly-scheduled meetings, such as those described by the team from Central Missouri State University, and sometimes participants exchange notes and drafts of documents when meeting time is scarce. Sometimes it just takes a longer, more concentrated work time to stimulate reflection, such as workshops and retreats that occurred as part of the *Teaching for Tomorrow* Project. But whatever the form, routines must be established to support the review of products and the reflection on processes. The commitment to these routines is positively related to the success of any institution's reform effort.

External Relationships

The stories from teacher education institutions in this volume relate how dynamic initiatives originating within individual states, certification bodies, and professional organizations had an impact upon their process of change. Although these initiatives were sometimes perceived as overwhelming and difficult to implement, they provided both a starting point and a model for restructuring the program. At Winston-Salem State University, in contrast, the impetus to change was internal, and they moved toward outcomes and assessment as a result of a self-study begun in 1988. Although different in source, these initiatives or mandates provided the stimulus for institutions to begin the review process and the revision of their programs.

In the case of the University of Northern Colorado, when the state mandated it to become Colorado's primary institution for graduate and undergraduate teacher education in 1986 (Rude), the education faculty were able to integrate their efforts in designing four new teacher preparation programs with the work they were already doing as part of Goodlad's National Network for Educational Renewal. The ability to coalesce multiple initiatives and find a common focus—in this case, the improvement of teacher education—was a critical factor in the University of Northern Colorado's program restructuring.

All three institutions in the *Teaching for Tomorrow* Project as well as Ashland University and Central Missouri State University were seeking NCATE accreditation during the time of their program revision. Without a doubt, the new NCATE standards served as a model for developing outcomes-based programs, and the impending site visits provided a stimulus for intense activity on each campus. The need was more acute for Clayton College & State University, who in addition to getting a new program up and off the ground had to secure unit accreditation before certifying its first set of program graduates. The need to develop a performance-based curriculum and an assessment program with which to judge its graduates pushed the college to maintain a high level of activity from preconditions to site visit as it addressed the state and national accreditation timelines.

The national standards in the content areas were instrumental in providing a framework for the design of individual courses and assessments in the teacher education programs. In both the P–12 and the higher education settings, educators moving from an input to an output model of performance were asking similar questions about the relationship between teaching and learning and curriculum and assessment. Heuwinkel and Hagerty observe that since the school-based faculty had already begun to implement standards-based assessment in their classrooms, they were a valuable resource to the University of Northern Colorado faculty who had little training or expertise in this area. Durden and Hunt relate how they relied heavily upon the national content standards in mathematics and language arts as well as guidelines for the development of middle school learners to design course content and assessment at Clayton College & State University.

Developing relationships with other institutions "in the same boat" is essential if one is to find the support and resources needed to maintain reform. But as teams become more sophisticated in their restructuring and more skillful in their redesign, the nature of the relationships changes. The three institutions of the *Teaching for Tomorrow* Project and their Alverno colleagues met together regularly to share what they had learned and to gain help and support from one another during the Annual Meetings of the AAHE Assessment Forum and of AACTE. At the beginning of the project, these meetings were characterized by teams hoping to find a "one-size-fits-all" formula that would ease their dilemmas with the design and implementation of standards, teaching, and assessment. But as their work advanced, each team came to realize that 1) their institution had a unique faculty, student body, and culture; 2) this uniqueness was its strength; and 3) other institutions' solutions could not be cut-and-pasted into their own without dire consequences. One institution's model of teaching, learning, and assessment cannot be mapped onto another institution's reform package; but other models do offer examples from which we can learn and see the complexities of the task before us.

Maintaining a relationship with outside consultants can be a significant factor in the success of restructuring efforts. Winston-Salem State University faculty relate how an outside consultant presented workshops to help them initiate the development of their critical thinking outcomes. At Central Missouri State University, a consultant helped a core committee conceptualize an outcomes-based program. But working with a consultant requires the institution to be open to what a consultant has to offer: the willingness of the *Teaching for Tomorrow* teams to accept technical support from the Alverno College team was essential to the success of that project.

The process of moving towards a standards-based teacher education program with a substantial assessment component either was done in tandem with these outside mandates or was initiated by the mandate itself. In either case, the institutions working through these changes were able to find a common link among the directives (often the need to develop outcomes or to move toward performance-based assessment) and to view them as an opportunity for program improvement.

Designing Processes That Support Change

While relationships are central to supporting change in teacher education, they are dependent upon processes to sustain that change. Here we address three processes that can serve to sustain the emerging standards-based thrust in teacher education: ways of thinking, ways of working, and ways of relating[1].

Ways of Thinking

From our work with higher education generally and with the *Teaching for Tomorrow* Project in particular, certain ways of thinking have emerged that support the necessary changes in programs that prepare teacher candidates. When teacher educators and other constituents engaged in innovative programs are *viewing change positively*, that positive attitude in itself supports the complex change process. It often serves to motivate a continuing focus on change as well. The "learning gyre" framework developed by faculty at Winston-Salem State University is a helpful illustration of this point. The gyre guided faculty to remember the cyclical, progressive, and recursive nature of change.

Taking multiple perspectives is a second way of thinking that supports change. When educators view an issue from several different angles, they more easily approach problems creatively to support deeper questioning and more appropriate solutions. No one entity has the expertise to accomplish changing teacher education. In the *Teaching for Tomorrow* Project, multiple perspectives were presented through the ongoing collaboration and commitment of Alverno faculty, education and arts and sciences faculty from participating institutions, and P–12 personnel through partner

---

[1]   In addition to the framework offered here, it is also helpful to refer to Harvey Rude's discussion of the change process at the University of Northern Colorado (UNC). He presents an extensive discussion of lessons learned as a result of major restructuring of the UNC teacher education program.

---

school participation at the project institutions. Through this multi-perspective dialogue, teams became aware of varying constituent needs and jointly developed processes to explore, evaluate, and prioritize those needs. Together each team strove then to design a program that best met those needs. Understanding emerged of the unique culture of each constituency; and allowing those cultures to co-exist encouraged the valuing of contributions of each in the process, initiated the appreciation of differences that arose, and caused progress to be made toward common goals.

A third way of thinking involves *accepting and appreciating two important realities* of restructured programs: 1) standards, frameworks, and courses and/or programs are not an add-on to business as usual; and 2) teaching is interactive with learning. The first reality is illustrated through the experience of faculty at the University of Northern Colorado. Heuwinkel and Hagerty state, "Faculty found that course topics that might once have been 'near and dear' to the heart had to be deleted if they did not fit with program outcomes." Linda Darling-Hammond points out the second reality in the dialogue on standards and assessment. She states, "Teaching is not just the formulaic demonstration of a set of 'canned' teaching behaviors, which are performed without attention to whether children are learning or not. New standards and assessments are beginning to make clear the connections between teaching as decision-making and learning."

Finally, disequilibrium occurs naturally in the midst of change because new ways of thinking about educating and new ways of expressing expectations force methods to change in ways that are neither predictable nor necessarily stable. Although it is potentially stressful, *valuing disequilibrium* is the fourth way of thinking that fosters change. Heuwinkel and Hagerty talk about the importance of recognizing the unpredictability of the process while still maintaining a focus on the goals for change. "Progression towards implementing standards has been nonlinear, with unexpected setbacks and unpredicted progress." The unpredicted progress that occurred through valuing disequilibrium helped partners in change to tolerate unanticipated setbacks.

Ways of Working

Once change has been initiated, constituents need to take responsibility for their growth and to develop a process to maintain that growth pattern over time. This way of working—*designing a continuous improvement model*—provides a way for faculty routinely to evaluate program progress. To prevent progress from being defined simply as "activity," the commitment to continuous change must be toward specific goals. At Central Missouri State University, faculty adopted a Continuous Process Improvement (CPI) project which redefined the institution's responsibility for student learning at the same time they were redesigning their teacher education program (Mihalevich & Carr). Faculty across the institution focused on teaching for student needs and monitoring student learning.

Communicating across stakeholders is a major factor in maintaining the focus on change. *Communicating effectively*, as a second way of working, challenges participants to identify issues that need to be resolved so that change continues. For example, as mentioned previously in this chapter, the *Teaching for Tomorrow* participants designed a meeting-within-a-meeting process. At national meetings such as AACTE and AAHE, they met to dialogue about common issues and to serve as resources to one another as their restructuring progressed.

Pacing the change process became another key practice, or third way of working, identified with the *Teaching for Tomorrow* Project. The combination of disequilibrium along with an awareness of the need to keep pressing forward guided participants to make significant change over time, while recognizing that the process for desired change itself takes patience to achieve its results. It was necessary to attend to the immediacy of the project—as new programs were implemented and courses taught—while maintaining a significant focus on the global, long-term efforts. At the same time, participants realized they needed to anticipate and accept the powerful commitment of energies and significant devotion of time that it took to accomplish the goals of designing strong standards-based teacher education programs; and they needed time to continue to be present in P–12 classrooms, to write about their experiences, to reflect on the processes of change, and to pursue related endeavors to strengthen their ability to contribute meaningfully to teacher education programs. When the elementary program faculty at the University of Northern Colorado began their work in professional development schools, they attempted also to continue their assessment committee work with the same level of intensity with which they began it. However, faculty soon admitted that they could no longer devote the same amount of time to assessment design as they had been and still maintain the necessary level of professionalism in their work with partner schools. They readjusted their priorities by deciding to dispense with assessment committee work for the first semester of the new program so that P–12 teachers and university faculty could devote attention to the program's successful implementation.

Creating a zone of comfort in the midst of change helps those engaged in change to keep an openness to continued refinement as the program develops and changes. Faculty move from questioning why they are engaging in the change process at all, given all of its real and potential frustrations, to finding ways to tolerate the messiness. Sometimes this means developing a willingness to postpone closure on an issue until faculty have experienced what it means to change. Schnug and Shelly talk about a "beneficial sense of unease" as faculty work through what it means to teach and assess from a conceptual framework. Or often, decisions need to be made on the scope of change, even to the point of eliminating a portion of the change plan so as to realistically meet the needs of the constituents, institution, or program. One of the lessons learned by the faculty engaged in reform at Central Missouri State University was to limit the scope of the project to maintain faculty interest and commitment, for in the words of Mihalevich and Carr, they "tackled too much at once," initially identifying too many outcomes without realizing the difficulty of the task.

A fifth way of working is *employing frameworks* as guides to the change process. Winston-Salem State University's learning gyre provided such a framework to its faculty. The tenets, benchmarks, and strands developed by Ashland University provide helpful examples of frameworks as effective guides. Their overall process of inquiry, implementation, and review is another useful framework. The University of Northern Colorado designed its four programs according to a set of stages or phases that students complete to guide them through the program. Frameworks, although serving different purposes, provide a structure for understanding, helping faculty and students to develop an explicit set of priorities and to anticipate next steps in the change/learning process.

Creating new norms that affect success in an institution is a sixth way of working. The practice of attending or not attending meetings, for example, can make a difference in faculty commitment to the process of change. At the University of Northern Colorado, P–12 faculty found it much easier than university faculty to remove themselves from the routine issues and spend a whole day on assessment development (Heuwinkel & Hagerty). Similarly, the degree of openness for discussion influences the nature of creativity of ideas in meetings. Furthermore, blind action can overtake a process where sufficient time for reflection is not provided. At Winston-Salem State University, the timeline for implementation was flexible, with adjustments reflecting faculty readiness to proceed (McCarter *et al.*). Finally, the consensus process can be delicate if no support process is also put in place. It may be necessary for an institution to mitigate its behavioral norms consciously as a part of or even as a precursor to the change process. This was certainly the case at Winston-Salem State University, where the planning team "realized that the shift to a outcomes-based learning model would necessarily involve 'changing the culture' of the campus," and that such a change would need to be carefully understood and implemented if the revision of the teacher education program was to be realized.

Ways of Relating

Ways of relating comprise the third and final process we address for sustaining change. One way of relating as teacher education programs evolve is for faculty to *learn to anticipate responses* by students as well as by faculty colleagues *to the change process* itself. It became important to acknowledge and diffuse the stress levels of students who questioned program changes in the *Teaching for Tomorrow* Project institutions, for example. Provisions for channeling questions were helpful, such as having students who had been through it help other students to anticipate and understand the change process, and to strategize ways to adjust. For faculty, creating ways of maintaining open communication and encouraging their involvement to share information and reactions fostered an openness to change and a desire to learn from one another.

Another way of relating is for change agents to *invite a wide range of faculty* to participate in designing courses and programs. Recognizing colleagues' expertise and seeking it out reinforces a collaborative culture and allows sometimes-reluctant colleagues to see the importance of their contribution to the whole. The University of Northern Colorado program designers formed an assessment committee by asking certain members of the education department faculty, arts and sciences faculty, and four teachers from partner schools to meet together on a regular basis to design assessment, for example.

A third way of relating is to *bring together all participants* in the process in a location apart from the usual. Retreats are powerful motivators for sustaining change. Retreats not only allow people to work uninterrupted by technology and daily routine, but they also provide opportunities for participants to celebrate and to view progress in a new light. A springtime retreat to Vail, Colorado by the *Teaching for Tomorrow* teams—including laboratory school teachers who work with the University of Northern Colorado faculty—provided such an opportunity to accomplish significant work on programs, share frustrations and successes, and rejuvenate.

A fourth way of relating is to *interact with outside consultants* brought to campus to utilize the power of fresh perspectives to rekindle progress and provide for a somewhat detached evaluation of the program. When Alverno faculty visited *Teaching for Tomorrow* teams, they not only lent a continuity of support while asking useful questions and making meaningful suggestions to support the teams' work, but also provided feedback that helped those teams better create their own success. The purpose of consultants is to help put the change process in motion, advance processes already in place, and provide fresh insights and objective feedback. The purpose of consultants is not to impose their own model of change without attention to the culture of the institution or to the goals of the change process itself.

Conclusion

Through this discussion of institutions involved in the process of change, we have highlighted two practices that support change in teacher education institutions: developing relationships—internal and external—and designing processes—ways of thinking, working, and relating—that foster successful standards-based teacher education programs. The stories in this volume testify to the difficulty and complexity of initiating and sustaining change. But they also demonstrate that the change process is a learning process, and that learning as we progress is really what helps us to become successful. It is that capacity on the part of everyone engaged in the process to learn on a continuous basis that, in the long run, sustains educational change.

■

Institutionalizing a Standards-Based Approach To Teaching, Learning, and Assessment

■

Kathryn Henn-Reinke and Kathleen M. Kies

In preceding sections of this monograph, it has been noted that writers from each contributing institution described disquieting levels of disequilibrium as reform efforts took faculty, staff, and school partners into uncharted waters at uneven rates of change. As new language and new processes emerged, more and more elements came into alignment with changed assumptions. Continuing discussions and experiences clarified specific areas where refinement was needed.

During the institutionalizing process, colleges and universities actually move into a period of "reculturation" in which the struggle to redefine themselves leads to a new identity. Development of a critical mass of students and faculty talking the same language and sharing the same assumptions supports the shift. This stage is characterized by a clarification of language among stakeholders involved in the process. Institutional structures and ways of doing business can be altered to assure that desired practices related to standards and assessments will remain, and continue to be developed.

Institutionalization must be a conscious and integral part of the entire change process, rather than an effort undertaken late and separately that attempts to build in persistence. The entire work of changing an institution or program requires an integration of the processes of creating a climate for change, changing, and institutionalizing the change, while maintaining continuous openness.

As we look at the experiences of these institutions, the process of institutionalizing has forced each of them to search for answers to the following questions:

- How can people institutionalize a new way of working in higher education that is collaborative and characterized by open communication in all directions?
- How can faculties and administrators sustain the continuing renewal process within their institutions, based on altered *assumptions, relationships,* and *practices*?

Institutionalize New Assumptions, A New Culture

An essential step in institutionalizing new assumptions is formal adoption of a restructured philosophical base that connects teaching, learning, standards, and assessment. As can be seen in the articles by Heuwinkel and Hagerty and by Rude, at the University of Northern Colorado (UNC) such a new philosophical base was institutionalized. Discrete new administrative structures called Professional Teacher Education Programs within a new School for the Study of Teaching and Teacher Education enabled focus of selected faculty on teaching and learning for the education of beginning teachers, within a larger College of Education. From Central Missouri State University (CMSU), Mihalevich and Carr write about the influence of Walter Deming's Total Quality Management (TQM), first on its College of Business and Economics, and then encompassing the entire university.

One of the common pitfalls that causes reform efforts to abort is that the changes that are made do not reflect substantive shifts in assumptions about how students learn, how student learning links with teaching, how theory relates to practice, or how changes in teaching and learning dictate reconceptualization of the process for assessing student progress. Even if such new assumptions are articulated, they may not be reflected in the formally adopted philosophy or mission statement of the institution. Rude writes of a "philosophy of reflective practice," of reconceiving program content as "integrated and coherent," and of accountability through performance assessment.

Some of the assumptions that guided work of the seven institutions have been re-articulated, or illustrated by changes in practice:

Assumed: The student's learning is central. When program design begins with the assumption that the student and learning are central, teaching and assessment become the mechanisms enabling progressive learning by every student, rather than mechanisms for sorting those who can from those who cannot. When the student's learning becomes the center of attention, faculty work is redesigned, as can be seen in the accounts by Nelms and Thomas and by Durden and Hunt of work done by language arts and mathematics faculty at Clayton College & State University (CCSU). When the focus within an institution changes from the number of courses offered and the content covered within those courses to actual student performance, all of the work within that institution gradually is changed or refined to match this new focus. In the Education Department at Asbury College, according to Lowe and Banker, the mission statement has been revised and the faculty are now charged with producing "teachers who are facilitators of student success." The education faculty have had to become models of such teaching as they reflect this philosophic shift.

Assumed: Assessment serves to diagnose further needs for learning and is a part of the teaching and learning process. When a faculty assumes that assessment is a diagnostic tool that enables further development, it begins adopting performance outcomes and criteria for the assessment of these outcomes. Pre-stated expectations give students a clear indication of how closely they approximate the standards set for successful participation in a profession—in this case, the teaching profession. Students begin carrying responsibility for their own learning, and the tasks of teaching change. As faculty become comfortable with new tasks, their perceptions of their own roles change, and new behaviors become the daily norm.

Assumed: Feedback enables students to learn to assess their own progress and to self-correct toward goals. Another changed assumption that indicates progress toward institutionalization of a standards-based curriculum is that feedback becomes a positive, indispensable part of the teaching, learning, and assessment process. Feedback to students enables them to focus on areas of strength and challenge, and assists them in setting goals. As this process becomes internalized, students view it as a natural part of all learning both in and outside the classroom. Preservice teachers view the provision of constructive feedback as part of their responsibility in helping children develop as fully as possible. College faculty view student feedback to course learning experiences and assessments as an invaluable tool to continually improve courses in a way that fosters coherent programs of student development toward goals and standards. And as all members of the circle—children, teachers, and college faculty—arrive at similar attitudes, it becomes progressively easier to act in accord with them.

Assumed: A teaching/learning organization functions optimally in the collaborative mode; teaching need not be a solitary, private occupation. When it is assumed that program responsibilities will be handled collaboratively, new teams such as Winston-Salem State University's satellite groups emerge and become regularized through use. Partnerships such as CCSU's between arts and sciences faculty and middle school practitioners become the norm rather than the exception. Time is found for faculty to meet in pursuit of a new mission, as at Ashland University or for all-day meetings and retreats as at UNC. Faculty not only serve on committees, but form program task groups or informal clusters to work on specific problems.

Assumed: State and national professional standards can serve as a template against which to check locally developed program outcomes for gaps or overlaps. It is easy to assume that meeting state and national standards that have been developed for teaching and for various academic disciplines such as science and mathematics is sufficient for development of new programs. Such standards frequently outline and describe what beginning practitioners should know, do, and be like to help ensure success in those fields. By adopting these as ways to structure the education curriculum and individual courses, institutions can see themselves as helping students gain expertise, and can be comfortably assured that they are educating professionals who are successful and are able to make positive contributions to the field of education. A changed assumption might indicate use of these standards as a check to assure completeness *after programs are developed.* Schnug and Shelly write that at Ashland, only after they had reconceptualized their program in a way that was consistent with their vision of reform did they consult educational standards for further development.

As faculty become more confident in "owning" their developed culture and internalize their new assumptions about teaching, learning, and assessment, the way in which they view external models also changes. As mentioned earlier, in initial stages of program change, models from other institutions and national or state bodies are often used as a sort of map to guide the work. But in institutionalization, external models begin to serve as integrity checks. The institution has defined itself clearly enough that fresh mandates are examined for philosophical "fit" and then adapted in ways that do not compromise the integrity of the new program and, indeed, build on its uniqueness. Confidence in what has been achieved thus far, and in the reformulated identity of a program or an institution, provides a new level of freedom. Once a faculty group has developed its own model, a collective "license for creativity" enables them to see themselves as their own best resource.

Assumed: Dewey was right! Doing and learning are connected. Every chapter yields evidence that an assumed connection between learning and doing leads to more frequent, as well as more carefully structured and jointly assessed, field experiences.

Assumed: An improved teacher education program depends on strong collaboration among arts and sciences, P–12, and education faculties. At CCSU, according to Nelms and Thomas, arts and sciences faculty and adjunct faculty members have assumed strong roles within the teacher education program. Consequently, the culture has begun to change: participants habitually put procedures and practices into place that facilitate flexibility in thinking, communicating, and implementing new ways of doing things on campus.

Institutionalize New Relationships

Shared understandings of a new culture of teaching, learning, and assessment can only emerge through ongoing, wide-ranging opportunities for discussion among potential stakeholders. Discourse serves as a catalyst for all subsequent change. McCarter *et al.* recognized the importance of cross-disciplinary discussion at Winston-Salem State University very early in the process. We have already noted that CCSU initiated discourse between arts and sciences faculty and middle school practitioners. UNC's Heuwinkel and Hagerty also recognized school personnel as partners in the discussion and facilitated release time for teachers and administrators to participate. Discussions have become vehicles for continual refinement of newly developed programs, as they are pilot-tested or fully implemented. Because institutions and departments experienced the richness of this eclectic approach, they searched for more permanent ways to maintain communication across traditional dividing lines. Some of those divisions may be between colleges in a large university, or between departments in a smaller institution, as well as between institutions of higher education and P–12 partners in practice.

Development of ongoing change mechanisms related to desired standards and their assessment must also take place in open conversations that include all stakeholders. Winston-Salem's satellite discussion groups balanced top-down influences with bottom-up initiatives across disciplines to keep many stakeholders involved. Potential leaders and supporters were invited to participate in key positions. Those who contributed or provided workshops about what they were doing became willing participants in the continuing process. Common goals, outcomes, language, and understandings have become the connecting links across the campus.

Leadership itself can shift between university and practitioners. UNC's new elementary education program has been jointly designed with partner school coordinators and teachers often taking the lead, according to Heuwinkel and Hagerty. Its laboratory school faculty, who have also embarked on program redesign and improved student assessment, have shared in the dialogue and have shared products as they have emerged.

As another example, Diez and Hass recapitulate how Alverno College has established departments for each of its eight abilities. Each faculty member belongs to a disciplinary department, and many also elect to belong to an "ability" department. Cross-disciplinary groups meet regularly to refine their understandings of the abilities and how these relate to the broader teaching/learning/assessment process. Opportunities are provided—through oral and written reports, workshops, and informal sessions—for these groups to share what they have learned with the entire faculty.

The joint development of courses and assessments assures adoption of coherent program outcomes within and across disciplines, as seen in the chapters by McCarter *et al.* and Rude. This collaborative effort cannot be over-emphasized as a prerequisite for institutionalizing changes. When faculty across disciplines participate in developing courses and assessments, program outcomes are more easily understood and implemented. A greater commitment to achieving outcomes is visible in every sector of the enterprise that has participated in developmental work. Although it proves cumbersome to collaborate on the development and revision of curricula, joint ownership is clearly necessary if innovations are to persevere in an institutional setting. Many informal communication mechanisms help with this process.

Each of the institutions in the *Teaching for Tomorrow* Project has developed new student handbooks that communicate expectations clearly. The clarification of language, in fact, reflects clarification of the new culture that has emerged through months and months of discussion and debate. Winston-Salem's publication of their Student Assessment for Teaching and Learning (SALT) document and Ashland's conceptual strands and tenets are two examples of the formalization of this process. These documents also serve as resources for integrating new faculty into the unique culture.

An important part of building a continuing culture is the acculturation of new members of the group, and of part-time faculty. In each of the four institutions of the *Teaching for Tomorrow* Project, changes of key team members have challenged the institutionalization process. Mentoring and special opportunities for inservice training of new people have helped, and can be an integral part of institutional culture. After all, academic changes of personnel are frequent, and a standards-based curriculum must continue beyond the professional life of a particular innovator in a particular institution.

Institutionalize New Practices in the Use of Time, Resources, and Institution-Wide Support

Changes that emerge from the need to meet accreditation or state-imposed standards or the goals of specific-purpose grants are often ephemeral. Special committees and assignments disappear after their purposes have been met, unless their work is seen as central to the institution.

Changes toward a more student-centered approach, especially as they are embraced by students, become reinforced and honored in institutional practice. Equally, changes rooted in faculty desires for meaningful achievement of a vision are more likely to become a part of daily functioning, or even, as Rude reports from UNC, published in the college bulletin after lengthy approval processes. Focus can then remain on goals, and not on resistances, problems, or maintenance of the *status quo*.

In recent tradition, universities and colleges have been organized by function, and administrative divisions placed in charge of what are seen as discrete tasks. Such assignments, especially in large institutions, lead to fragmentation of effort. A standards-driven institution will likely seek greater integration of all of the efforts of staff and faculty toward desired outcomes. Old divisions of labor may be replaced by new task forces or internal structures. At Ashland University, standing committees were reconstituted with specific charges derived from the newly designed tenets and abilities.

"Systems" Perspective on Practices

From a "systems" perspective, a change in one part of a program will cause changes in other areas. As newly designed programs become institutionalized, it is important to ensure that all of the components of the program remain compatible and lead students more directly to the abilities highlighted in the standards. Participants put new procedures and practices into place that facilitate flexibility in thinking, communicating, and implementing new ways of doing business on campus. *Voila*—the culture changes!

Formal Statements Reflected in Funding Allocations

An institution of education, in practice, manages time, space, material, and human resources toward its publicly avowed goals. Thus, to institutionalize change, and to build in ways to continue the process of change, some formal avowal of philosophy or mission or goals may be needed. Then, as indications of the value placed on a changed culture, it is possible to create different ways to use these resources. Money and its allocation merely reflect cultural values as an instrumentality used to provide human resources, and to buy and equip spaces in new ways, to accomplish goals more directly.

Values Reflected in Time Allocations

Time for program design and for experimentation is a necessary element of change. Funds are needed to reimburse faculty and staff for time devoted to the ongoing development of outcomes-focused curricula outside of their regularly scheduled responsibilities, both within and outside of standard academic calendars. Often, the most feasible time for faculty to work at such major projects is during summer work sessions, retreats, or release time during the academic year. Time of support staff and partner school staff can often be purchased, as described by Rude at UNC.

Time is only of value if the energies of appropriate and committed people—including faculty, support staff, administrators, and students—can be shared in groups that are directly related to the goals and outcomes sought, whether these goals are development of new programs, reconceptualized courses, new assessments, new methods of keeping records, or new ways to aid students as they strive toward attainment of standards. Faculty, staff, and administrators need opportunities to reflect, refine, or reexamine outcomes, learning experiences, and assessments with colleagues. If such reflection and joint effort is perceived as an important element of faculty work, it can take precedence over other activities. Providing funds that allow in-depth focus on such tasks signals values held by senior administrators. Especially notable was the amount of time and the frequency and regularity of meetings allotted at Ashland.

In addition to finding ways to allot time for collaborative efforts by faculty, classroom and examination times can be reexamined. For example, if one desired outcome is that students become proficient communicators, as at Alverno, faculty must have sufficient time to determine how this ability can best be developed across the curriculum, to identify the types of learning experiences that will enable students to develop this expertise, and to assess and receive feedback on the effectiveness of the new learning experiences. Time must be allotted for the practice of the skills, student self-assessment, student reception of feedback, and student refinement of skills.

Values Reflected in Rewards

Faculty reward systems are part of this same fabric. The kind of energy required to redesign entire programs has not, in recent history, been seen as worthy of reward in faculty retention, promotion, and tenure systems. Linking promotion to the work of restructuring reinforces the notion that faculty work in this area is of critical importance to the functioning of the institution and supports practices that place students at the center of the curriculum. Although pursuit of a vision, participation on a team, recognition of one's ideas through publication, and enlightened self-interest are sometimes powerful incentives, efforts toward better ways of helping students learn and achieve also require positive, concrete rewards if they are to persist.

Values Reflected in Allotments of Space and Equipment

Funds are also, of course, used to buy and equip spaces—classrooms, libraries, gymnasia, laboratories, and offices—within which to conduct the enterprise of teaching and learning. Providing spaces and equipping them with technology that is both necessary and sufficient for achievement of a particular outcome frequently calls for practices that are creative and flexible, and for willingness to learn and to share.

In some instances, reconceptualizing the traditional use of existing space will be required as well. Space used for very specific purposes can be assigned with greater flexibility. Proprietorship or automatic assignment of rooms/space can be reexamined in face of the need for expanded usage.

Other institutional procedures, such as scheduling of classes and assessments or review periods, are often regarded as immutable. As new learning approaches are institutionalized, these practices must serve desired learning outcomes. Traditions regarding registration, advising, and graduation may be revised during the institutionalizing process. Feedback and advising have become inseparably integrated at Alverno, for example. General advising sessions have been created prior to registration to guide students in the selection of courses within the education sequence. In reality, very few institutional schedules are sacred. A calendar designed in the era of an agricultural America may no longer meet the needs of newly emergent nontraditional student populations. Weekly class schedules that offer intervals between instructional episodes in which reflection can take place may be superseded by more compact and intense learning experiences for students with different learning styles or needs.

Institutionally budgeted funds can be reallocated in all of these different ways, to assure that the institution's practices help to achieve desired learning outcomes. This does not negate the need for continued search for specialized funds to augment ongoing development of the program(s).

All of the practices discussed here reflect most concretely on an institution's values. As these practices change, it becomes increasingly evident that the institution itself or its teacher education program is committed to a continuing change process.

Conclusion

Perhaps most difficult for an institution is to understand and develop its culture—its prevailing attitudes. The institutions represented in this monograph have undertaken this difficult task. Institutional norms of practice are changing at all of them—and at many others.

The changed structures discussed above are not easily accomplished. Budgets, positions, and tasks are not easily relinquished. Course content is difficult to compress or surrender. Unhindered, courses continually expand and even proliferate! Program structures are seen as hallowed by time and usage. Often change is seen as an additive process, so that programs become cumbersome and lose coherence and integration.

It has been necessary for the institutions in this monograph to examine and seek to change those attitudes that presented obstacles to reforming teacher education programs. They have needed to assure that the process of development continues when external stimuli and funds have vanished. They appear prepared to remain focused on clarifying teaching and learning goals, and then mobilizing all resources toward achieving those goals. They have developed structures for communication regarding shared visions, and for implementing their new visions.

Attitudes can be changed either through incentives or through disincentives. More powerful change can occur with the use of incentives—and not always monetary ones. Perceived institutional response to the changing needs of students and faculty is a powerful motivator. Perceived student response also is a powerful motivator.

Institutionalizing not a specific change, but the change process, is the goal. Alverno College, Asbury College, Ashland University, Central Missouri State University, Clayton College & State University, the University of Northern Colorado, and Winston-Salem State University are engaged in an odyssey of continual reexamination. They keep on keeping on, in the sure knowledge that our society and its institutions are dynamic, that the vigor of our enterprise is best served by frequent and regular self-assessment, that renewal is never finished, but that this reform is securely grounded in best practice and the best thinking of scholars and researchers.

ABOUT THE CONTRIBUTORS

∎

Bonnie J. Banker, professor of education, teaches at Asbury College in Wilmore, Kentucky, in the areas of reading assessment, foundations in education, and supervision of field experience. She has chaired several committees at the Kentucky Department of Education as they pursue reform.

Carolynn B. Berry is associate professor and chairperson of the Department of Physical Education at Winston-Salem State University in Winston-Salem, North Carolina. She has chaired the faculty evaluation committee for several years and served on the University of North Carolina's committee to study post-tenure review.

Barbara Burch is provost and vice president for academic affairs at Western Kentucky University. A former dean of education, she is a past president of AACTE with experience on several standards and policy boards.

Ruby E. Burgess is professor and chairperson of the Department of Education at Winston-Salem State University in Winston-Salem, North Carolina. She is a specialist in curriculum development and diversity education and has served as a consultant to school districts and institutions of higher education.

Kathryn S. Carr, professor of reading, teaches literacy and literature methods courses in the Department of Curriculum and Instruction at Central Missouri State University in Warrensburg, Missouri. She has been active in developing the university-wide student outcomes and performance assessment.

Linda Darling-Hammond is William F. Russell Professor in the Foundations of Education at Teachers College, Columbia University, where she is also co-director of the National Center for Restructuring Education,

---

Schools, and Teaching (NCREST). A member of the National Board for Professional Teaching Standards and chair of the Model Standards Committee for INTASC, she also serves as executive director of the National Commission on Teaching & America's Future.

Mary E. Diez, chair of the Division of Education at Alverno College from 1985-1997, and now professor of education and director of the Master of Arts in Education at the college, directed the *Teaching for Tomorrow* Project. A former AACTE president, she is a member of the NCATE Board of Examiners, serves on the Model Standards Committee and the Technical Advisory Committee for INTASC, and is a member of the National Board for Professional Teaching Standards.

Debra Durden, assistant professor of English at Clayton College & State University in Morrow, Georgia, and former public school educator, has been closely involved with the development of the middle grades teacher education program at CCSU.

Patricia J. Hagerty is associate professor and director of the University of Colorado at Denver Literacy Consortium. She is an associate of the Institute for Educational Inquiry in Seattle and works with partner schools at the University of Colorado.

Jacqueline M. Hass, associate professor of education at Alverno College in Milwaukee, Wisconsin, teaches technology, integrated language arts, and curriculum courses. She works with both P–12 and teacher education institutions in developing outcomes and program assessments.

Kathryn Henn-Reinke, associate professor of education at Alverno College in Milwaukee, Wisconsin, teaches courses in the areas of bilingual education and literacy learning. She also serves as a consultant for the development and implementation of assessment portfolios in several Milwaukee public schools.

Mary Heuwinkel is a doctoral candidate in elementary education at the University of Northern Colorado. As a graduate assistant, she facilitated the development of the performance assessment plan for the Elementary Professional Teacher Education Program at the university.

Annita Hunt, assistant professor of mathematics at Clayton College & State University in Morrow, Georgia, and former public school educator, has been closely involved with the development of the middle grades teacher education program at CCSU.

David G. Imig is the chief executive officer of the American Association of Colleges for Teacher Education. A leader in national and international teacher education, he is also a member of numerous standards and education policy boards.

Kathleen M. Kies, executive director emeritus of the New Mexico Commission on Higher Education, works in a variety of capacities with her adopted colleagues at Alverno College in Milwaukee, Wisconsin.

Verna J. Lowe, associate professor of education, teaches at Asbury College in Wilmore, Kentucky, in the areas of learning performance and assessment, exceptional learners, and technology in education. She currently serves as chair of the education department.

Shirley F. Manigault is professor and chairperson in the Department of English at Winston-Salem State University in Winston-Salem, North Carolina, where she teaches courses in British literature and literacy theory.

Merdis T. McCarter is professor of mathematics and chairperson of the Department of Mathematics at Winston-Salem State University in Winston-Salem, North Carolina. Her research focuses on educational change, faculty development, and general education program assessment.

Carol D. Mihalevich, associate professor of reading, teaches literacy methods courses in the Department of Curriculum and Instruction at Central Missouri State University in Warrensburg, Missouri. She has chaired the College of Education and Human Services Assessment Committee and currently chairs the Faculty Senate University Assessment Council.

Pamela Moss is associate professor in the School of Education at the University of Michigan. A member of the Board of Directors for the National Council on Measurement in Education, she is co-chair of the Technical Advisory Committee for INTASC's Assessment Development Project and a member of the technical advisory groups for the National Board for Professional Teaching Standards and the statewide assessment programs in California and New York.

Virginia C. Nelms, professor of education and coordinator for middle-level education, teaches at Clayton College & State University in Morrow, Georgia, where she works with arts and sciences faculty and site-based educators in the continuing development of the Middle-Level Teacher Education Program.

Raymond L. Pecheone is chief of the Bureau of Research and Teacher Assessment for the Connecticut State Department of Education, which has been a national leader in performance- based assessment work. He also serves on the Model Standards Committee and the Technical Advisory Committee for INTASC.

Diana Pullin is professor of Education Law and Public Policy at Boston College and coordinator of the Joint Degree Program in Law and Education. A former practicing attorney and dean of education, her research interests include educational evaluation and testing, equity, and public policy. She also has been an advisor to INTASC.

Harvey Rude is professor of special education at the University of Northern Colorado where he presently serves as director of the School for the Study of Teaching and Teacher Education. His research interests include professional development, partnerships, teacher leadership, and systems change.

William D. Schafer is professor in the Department of Measurement, Statistics, and Evaluation in the College of Education at the University of Maryland-College Park. Widely published in the area of assessment education, he was a member of the committee that drafted the *Code of Professional Responsibilities in Educational Measurement*, a statement of the National Council on Measurement and Education (NCME), and chaired an NCME committee that studied assessment education for teachers.

James Schnug is an associate professor in the Education Department at Ashland University in Ashland, Ohio, in the area of literacy learning. He has also worked as a teacher leader and site coordinator in the Reading Recovery program and currently oversees the university's Becker Reading Center.

Subash M. Shah is associate professor of political science and chairperson of the Department of Social Sciences at Winston-Salem State University in Winston-Salem, North Carolina. One of his substantive interests involves problems of organizational culture and transformation.

Ann Converse Shelly, professor and chair of the Education Department, teaches at Ashland University in Ashland, Ohio, in the areas of methods and foundations. She has worked with state departments of education and with NCATE as they have approached reform.

Julie A. Stoffels, assistant dean and director of teacher education at Western Michigan University in Kalamazoo, Michigan, was associate professor and coordinator of secondary education at Alverno College when she served on the Alverno *Teaching for Tomorrow* team.

Marilyn G. Thomas, instructor of teacher education and coordinator for field experiences at Clayton College & State University in Morrow, Georgia, is currently on a leave of absence while working with the State of Georgia Professional Standards Commission.

Leona C. Truchan, professor of biology at Alverno College in Milwaukee, Wisconsin, served as a liberal arts member on the Alverno *Teaching for Tomorrow* team. She is active locally and nationally in P–16 science education.

Lelia L. Vickers is chair of the Division of Education at Winston-Salem State University in North Carolina. She has served on the AACTE Committee on Accreditation and Board of Directors as well as on the NCATE Board of Examiners and the Unit Accreditation Board.

■